TOM JONES

NOTES

including

- *Life and Backgr*
- *List of Character*
- *Summaries and (*
- *Character Analy.*
- *General Commer*
- *Review Question*
- *Bibliography*

by
James C. Evans, Ph.*
Department of Englis*
University of British*

Editor

Gary Carey, M.A.
University of Colorado

Consulting Editor

James L. Roberts, Ph.D.
Department of English
University of Nebraska

Cliffs Notes, Inc.   Lincoln, Nebraska

CONTENTS

Tom Jones Notes

LIFE AND BACKGROUND

Tom Jones, a book of much vitality, hilarity, and charm, reflects both the comic vision of life and the intense social concern of its author. Henry Fielding was born on April 22, 1707, at Sharpham Park in Somersetshire to well-situated, upper-class parents. His mother was the granddaughter of Sir Henry Gold, Baron of the Exchequer, and his father, Edmund, fought against the forces of Louis XIV under the Duke of Marlborough, eventually rising to the rank of lieutenant-general. Fielding was educated first at home (much like Tom Jones) under the tutelage of a clergyman, then at Eton, and finally at the University of Leyden, which he attended from the spring of 1728 to the fall of 1729. Fielding, however, began his literary career even before he entered Leyden. And he began not as a novelist, but as a playwright: his first play, *Love in Several Masques*, was written and performed in the early months of 1728. During the next ten years, Fielding wrote eight long plays and more than fifteen short plays, which he called farces. Arthur Murphy, who wrote the first biography of Fielding in 1762, has summarized this achievement most tactfully:

> For though it must be acknowledged that in the whole collection there are few plays likely to make any considerable figure on the stage hereafter, yet they are worthy of being preserved, being the works of a genius, who, in his wildest and most inaccurate productions, yet occasionally displays the talents of a master.

All of the plays are comedies and most of them have a satirical edge. Apparently all of Fielding's plays were performed at least once, and the majority of them were at least moderately successful. Those most frequently read now are his final two plays, *Pasquin* (1736) and *The Historical Register of 1736* (1737), both of which illustrate Fielding's keen sense of his social milieu. In fact, the performance of *The Historical Register*, a satire on contemporary politicians, was perhaps the major cause of the passing of the Licensing Act of 1737 which limited the number of theaters and prohibited the performance of plays which, as Murphy phrases it, "publicly mimicked" the king or any of his officials.

The student of Fielding's novels should immediately recognize the influence of the dramatic form. The novels all illustrate three important traits undoubtedly learned on the stage: a facility with dialogue, an ability to structure fiction, and an amazingly dextrous handling of complicated plots.

In 1737, Fielding began to study law in the Middle Court and was admitted to the bar in 1740. Throughout the remaining fourteen years of his life, Fielding, besides writing four novels, three volumes of *Miscellanies*, political pamphlets, and publishing a biweekly newspaper, the *Covent Garden Journal*, was active both in his law practice and in social causes generally. His success in law is indicated by the fact that in 1748 he was named Justice of the Peace for the Westminster district of London and, in 1749, for the entire county of Middlesex. His last five years were spent in arduous, time-consuming work for social reform in both the courts and the streets of London. In January, 1753, he published a tract, "Proposal for Making an Effectual Provision for the Poor," and in the latter part of that year, he successfully executed a plan for decreasing crime in London. Unfortunately, his health suffered as a result of his endeavors, and in April, 1754, he was finally forced to resign his position as magistrate and move to Lisbon, where he died in October of that year. Fielding's social concerns are reflected throughout his novels, which chronicle eighteenth-century English social history and sharply portray various social evils of the era. This is particularly evident in his last novel, *Amelia* (1751), in which he lashed out against such things as the poorly written English debt laws and the lamentable state of English prisons. In *Tom Jones*, Fielding is concerned with the effects of the social vices of hypocrisy and vanity, though his approach here is much more light-hearted and amiable than in *Amelia*. As Fielding states in the dedicatory letter of *Tom Jones*, ". . . I have employed all the wit and humour of which I am master in the following history; wherein I have endeavored to laugh mankind out of their favourite follies and vices." This statement contains an indication of the serious matter of the book and the healthy, delightfully funny manner in which Fielding points to human error. He does not once move into Swiftian indignation, but attempts to correct us by making us laugh at ourselves.

Fielding's career as a novelist began at roughly the same time as his law practice. Though there is still some debate on the matter, most critics assume that Fielding wrote *Shamela* (1741) to parody *Pamela* (1740), a novel by a contemporary writer, Samuel Richardson. Both books are written as a series of letters from the heroine to various acquaintances. Fielding found both Richardson's attitude and Pamela's virtue, to say the least, rather pretentious, so he created Shamela not as a distressed maiden, but more like a *femme fatale* who schemes to satisfy her lusty nature and to marry well. The full subtitle of Fielding's book indicates both the tone and the content of *Shamela:*

> An Apology for the Life of Mrs. Shamela Andrews. In which, the many notorious Falshoods and Misrepresentations of a Book called *Pamela,* are exposed and refuted; and all the matchless Arts of that young Politician, set in a true and just light. Together with a full Account of all that passed between her and Parson Arthur Williams; whose Character is represented in a manner something different from what he bears in *Pamela.* The whole being exact Copies of authentic Papers delivered to the Editor.

The book was published under the pseudonym, Conny Keyber. Fielding wrote a second, more significant, parody of the same novel in 1742, *Joseph Andrews.* Richardson's novel tells of the efforts of a servant, Pamela Andrews, to escape her master's amorous advances. In Fielding's parody, Joseph Andrews, Pamela's brother, is forced to protect his virtue from attacks made by the mistress of the house, Lady Booby and by her attendant, Mrs. Slipslop. Fortunately, both for the novel and for literary history, *Joseph Andrews* is much more than a deflation of Richardson's pomposity and, when reading the novel, one must readily admit that parody is at least a secondary matter in the over-all plan of the novel. Although Fielding may be parodying Richardson, he is also satirizing human foibles, what Fielding referred to as "the true ridiculous."

More important, in *Joseph Andrews* we can see the testing ground for many of the techniques Fielding was to employ masterfully in *Tom Jones.* There are obvious structural parallels between the two novels. Both have a tightly-knit, complex, and rapidly moving plot, narrated by a fully-realized and always amusing *persona.* Both Tom and Joseph are unjustly forced from their homes and onto the road, where they meet numerous adventures. Both novels are picaresque and based on the pattern of Miguel Cervantes' seventeenth-century novel, *Don Quixote,* in which the plot concerns the travels of a hero and his companion and the various encounters on their journey. As is true of its occurrence in most pieces of literature, Tom's journey is more than just an account of his travels: it becomes symbolic of an Everyman's experience of life itself and, as such, is indicative of Fielding's own world view. In broad terms, we can see that *Tom Jones* basically concerns the continuing battle between virtue and vice, good and evil. Both novels have the same circular movement from the country to the road, to the city and back to the country.

For Fielding, who knew London intimately, the country, where the natural world is least affected by the coverings of civilization, is the home of ethical goodness. It contains, for example, the Eden-like sanctuary of Squire Allworthy's home. The city, with its crowded streets and abundance of crime and prisons, is the nesting place of evil. The road, which connects the two, is the place of battle between them. This kind of observation is much more significant on the symbolic level than on the literal: Tom's journey is representative of his process of maturation, the movement from innocence to experience; his return to the country marks the ultimate triumph of his basically good nature over his inclinations toward imprudent and rash actions. Finally, in both *Tom Jones* and *Joseph Andrews*, the resolution of the plot is brought about by a kind of *deus ex machina* which sets everything right: Joseph suddenly learns that his real father is a wealthy, landed gentleman; Tom's true parentage is disclosed. Virtue receives its reward. A further ramification of these conclusions is that they illustrate a major motif of both books, the quest for a father-figure. In the contexts of the novels this is easily explained: the father is the prime figure of authority. With the return of authority or, more aptly, *true* authority, we move out of the threatening world of the chaos of unethical, destructive action and back into the security of impartial justice and the warmth of paternal love. This is also the basic theme of the "divine comedy" of the Christian world view: man is born into the dire struggle of the temporal world (the road in *Tom Jones)* and, if he is worthy, he is at last restored to the protective arms of a benevolent God. In one sense, then, the novel is highly moral because it reflects the prime ethic of its social milieu.

However, *Joseph Andrews* and *Tom Jones* have a more significant relationship to each other and to the English novel generally. They mark the articulation and execution of a new theory of writing. The articulation of this theory is begun in Fielding's preface to *Joseph Andrews* and is continued in the introductory chapters of each of the eighteen books of *Tom Jones*.

In his preface to *Joseph Andrews,* Fielding defines the genre of his work, a "kind of writing which I do not remember to have seen hitherto attempted in our language," as the comic prose epic. As stated earlier, his immediate source of inspiration was the Spanish classic, *Don Quixote*. But in discussing his work, Fielding refers to Homer and Aristotle, the former for practice and the latter for theory. This kind of appeal to authority was extremely important during the Neo-Classical Age (1700-50). The classification is most apt, for this is the period of literary history in which writers and critics based their views of literature on classical figures, most important of whom were Homer and Aristotle. Alexander Pope has succinctly stated the prevailing view in one of the couplets from his *Essay on Criticism:*

> Learn hence for ancient rules a just esteem;
> To copy nature is to copy them.

Fielding states that he calls his work a *comic* epic because in every way it follows the epic form as written by Homer, except that it presents actions which are light and ridiculous rather than highly serious. It also introduces characters of inferior rank, its diction contains burlesque or is mock-heroic, and it is written in prose rather than verse. Further, the work imitates nature; that is, it reproduces what is observable in the environment and presents a hero of great significance successfully meeting supremely difficult tasks. In *Tom Jones,* Fielding presents us with a picture of man maintaining his essential goodness and humanity in spite of a world teeming with temptations and self-centered opportunists. What could be more ordinary and, at the same time, more significant?

But Fielding, ever able to see the ridiculous, does not fail to see the humor of critical categorizing and, in the first chapter of Book V of *Tom Jones,* he anticipates his literary critics. In answering the question of why he has a seemingly digressive preface to each section of his novel, Fielding writes:

> For this our determination we do not hold ourselves strictly bound to assign any reason, it being abundantly sufficient that we have laid it down as a rule necessary to be observed in all prosai-comi-epic writing. . . . It seems perhaps difficult to conceive that any one should have had enough of impudence to lay down dogmatical rules in any art or science without the least foundation. In such cases, therefore, we are apt to conclude there are sound and good reasons at the bottom, though we are unfortunately not able to see so far.

The tongue-in-cheek tone here is very reminiscent of Shakespeare's poke at the critics in *Hamlet.* Shakespeare is ridiculing critics when he has Polonius state that the actors who are about to perform are "the best actors in the world, either for tragedy, comedy, history, pastoral, pastoral-comical, historical-pastoral, tragical-historical, tragical-comical-historical-pastoral, scene individable or poem unlimited." Perhaps Fielding had these lines in mind when he called his new genre the "prosai-comi-epic."

Fielding also defines for us the central subject matter of his book: pretension and affectation unveiled,which he claims is "the only source of the true ridiculous." In the eighteen prefatory chapters of *Tom Jones*, Fielding reiterates the theory of his new genre. In the first chapter of Book I, using the now well-known menu metaphor, he reasserts the Aristotelian doctrine of imitation, stating that his "Bill of Fare" is "Human Nature," from the lowly servant to the lordly squire. In Book IX, he reaffirms the necessity for an artist to keep nature continually before him; in Books X and XI, he exhorts the critic to unchain himself from dogmatic rules and to consider the work as an organic piece of art, self-contained and self-justified. Taken together, these chapters are Fielding's plea for freedom from the complete dependence on rules to judge literature and a protestation that his "new province" is worthy to be considered on its own merits and should not be discarded because it does not fit into a prescribed mold.

One should not, however, get the impression that these prefatory chapters are restricted to literary discussions. They also contain discourses on love (Book VI), on the similarity between the world and the stage (Book VII), and on virtue (Book XV). Above all, they indicate Fielding's marvelous sense of humor and his penetrating insight into the human character.

LIST OF CHARACTERS

Squire Allworthy

A wealthy and wise landowner, magistrate, and philanthropist residing in Somersetshire, England.

Bridget Allworthy

The matronly sister of Squire Allworthy; she has little to recommend her but her wealth. She is, we finally learn, Tom's real mother.

Deborah Wilkins

The waiting-woman to Bridget and a self-styled overseer of the squire's manor and the morals of the family.

Tom Jones

The hero of the novel; he is the illegitimate son of Bridget. Allworthy adopts Tom and, even though he does not know that Tom is really his nephew, he treats him as if he were his own son.

Jenny Jones

An intelligent servant in the home of the schoolmaster, she is accused of being Tom's mother. For her own good, Allworthy reprimands her and sends her out of the neighborhood. She takes another name, Mrs. Waters, and Tom, after rescuing her, has a brief but intense affair with her at Upton Inn.

Mr. Partridge

The schoolmaster; he is timid, superstitious, beset with a shrewish wife and falsely accused of being Tom's father. When Tom later meets him, he has taken another name, Little Benjamin. After they discover each other's identity, Partridge decides to accompany Tom.

Captain Blifil

A hypocritical fortune seeker who pretends to virtue while taking advantage of Allworthy's hospitality and Bridget's natural instincts. Hoping to inherit the estate, he marries Bridget, but dies soon after their first child is born.

Master Blifil

The villainous son of Bridget and Captain Blifil. Like his father, he hopes to rule the entire Allworthy estate and therefore does everything in his power to see that Tom is disowned by Allworthy.

Mr. Thwackum

The devout Anglican parson whom Allworthy brings in to tutor Blifil and Tom. He is known for his ingratiating manner and his belief in the efficacy of the strap in educating children.

Mr. Square

The deist philosopher who, with Thwackum, is responsible for educating Allworthy's boys.

Squire Western

Allworthy's neighbor; he ardently loves three things: the hunt, the bottle, and his daughter, and probably in that order.

Sophia Western

The lovely, intelligent, and virtuous daughter of the squire; she is loved by Tom and his attempt to gain her hand forms the framework of the action in the novel. (Incidentally, many critics believe that the portrait of her in *Tom Jones* is Fielding's tribute to his own wife, who died in 1744. See Chapter II, Book IV.)

Mrs. Western

The commanding, stubborn, and pretentious sister of Squire Western. She has no husband or children of her own and therefore throws all of her energies along these lines onto Sophia and the squire.

Mrs. Honour

Sophia's servant; she helps Sophia to escape from her father's demand that she marry Blifil and accompanies her to London.

Parson Supple

The local Anglican parson and particular friend of Squire Western. He uses diplomacy on numerous occasions to calm the squire.

"Black George" Seagrim

An impoverished father of a fairly large family. He serves, on and off, as Squire Western's gamekeeper and attendant. Tom befriends George and gives him money and food to help sustain his family.

Molly Seagrim

George's daughter; she is renowned for her lax morals. Before Tom falls in love with Sophia, he has an affair with Molly—as does Mr. Square.

Lawyer Dowling

The lawyer whom Bridget hires to handle her estate and who is with her when she dies. He is one of three people in the novel who know the secret of Tom's birth, so Mr. Blifil makes sure that Dowling does not inadvertently reveal it.

Ensign Northerton

The soldier who taunts Tom about Sophia and finally hits him with a bottle of wine. He is also the scoundrel from whom Tom rescues Mrs. Waters later in the novel.

The Man of Mazard Hill

The self-exiled and bitter recluse whom Tom saves from being beaten and robbed. In return, Tom asks to hear the story of the man's life.

Sir George Gresham

The Man of the Hill's university cohort, who virtually led him into a life of debauchery.

Mr. Watson

The Man of the Hill's gambling companion in London.

Harriet Fitzpatrick

Sophia's cousin. Sophia meets her while they are both journeying to London. Harriet is escaping from a domineering and cruel husband; Sophia is fleeing from her father. They have that, as well as the fact that they once lived together with their mutual aunt, Mrs. Western, in common.

Mr. Fitzpatrick

A man rather like Captain Blifil in that he woos and marries a woman, Harriet, only for her money; before the wedding he is the picture of gentility, but turns out later to be totally self-centered.

The Irish Peer

Harriet Fitzpatrick's neighbor and friend in Ireland· he helps her escape from her husband and later becomes her lover.

Mrs. Miller

A widow of a clergyman, she now runs a boardinghouse in London. Allworthy has befriended her and Tom stays at her home when he arrives in London. She is a good and virtuous woman.

Nancy Miller

Mrs. Miller's daughter. She becomes the lover of one of her mother's tenants, Mr. Nightingale, whom she eventually marries.

Mr. Nightingale

A boarder at Mrs. Miller's home and "a man of wit and pleasure." He is Nancy Miller's lover and, after overcoming his father's demand that he marry for money, he marries Nancy, who is carrying his child.

Lady Bellaston

The extremely wealthy and debauched matron in London who takes Tom in and, for awhile, favors him with her gifts and herself.

Lord Fellamar

An English peer and friend of Lady Bellaston's; he falls in love with Sophia and attempts various ruses, including rape, to get her to marry him.

Mr. Summer

He is the son of a clergyman and a friend of Allworthy's who lives at the Allworthy estate for about a year, but dies about six months before Tom is born. It is he, so we learn at the end of the novel, who is Tom's real father.

SUMMARIES AND COMMENTARIES

BOOK I

Summary

The narrator introduces us to Squire Allworthy, one of the richest and most benevolent men in England. After the death in infancy of his three children and the death of his wife, he now lives with his maiden sister, Bridget. Squire Allworthy, returning from a lengthy business trip to London, finds a baby in his bed and commands an elderly servant, Mrs. Deborah Wilkins, to provide for it until morning. At breakfast the next morning, Allworthy announces his intention to keep the child and rear him as his own son. Mrs. Wilkins is given the task of inquiring throughout the parish to discover the child's mother. Miss Bridget is left with the responsibility of seeing to the child's needs and "her orders [are] indeed so liberal, that, had it been a child of her own, she could not have exceeded them."

Mrs. Wilkin's mission is most successful for, after conferring with another elderly matron, she accuses Jenny Jones of being the illegitimate child's mother. The logic behind the accusation is a bit odd: Jenny is out of favor with her neighbors because, as a servant in the house of the schoolmaster, she acquired an impressive education for one of her social rank. As a result, her peers envy and scorn her. The scorn, however, turned to derision recently when she appeared one Sunday in a rather showy, expensive gown, one which she could hardly have bought for herself. Also, as nurse to Bridget, she was recently in Allworthy's home. Regardless of the meager evidence, Jenny confesses to being the culprit. Mrs. Wilkins then takes her to Squire Allworthy, but not until she has given Jenny a severe tongue lashing, augmented by jeers from the crowd which has gathered.

Squire Allworthy lives up to his name; in his position as magistrate, he is lenient with Jenny. He reminds her of the consequences of her sin, both in this world and the next, and, in order to help her escape the condemnation of the villagers, he decides to send her to a part of the country where she will be unknown. All he asks is that she tell him the name of the child's father. Jenny, after expressing her gratitude, says she cannot tell because she is bound by the solemn oath of her honor and religion to keep his name concealed. But she does promise that Allworthy will one day learn the father's identity. Allworthy accepts this and concludes his admonishings with, "Consider, child, there is One still to reconcile yourself to, whose favour is of much greater importance to you than mine."

During this lecture, Miss Bridget and Mrs. Wilkins have been listening intently at the door of the squire's study, as they do frequently. Upon hearing the sentence, Mrs. Wilkins denounces Allworthy's leniency with such harlots. Miss Bridget, however, smiles and commends both Jenny for her honor and spirit and Allworthy for his mercy. Mrs.

Wilkins, of course, readily agrees with her and begins to lambast the roguery and inconstancy of villainous men.

As soon as the villagers, who had expected Jenny to be sent to the House of Correction, learn of Allworthy's decision, they once again scoff at Jenny and at Allworthy for playing favorites. And it is not long before they accuse Allworthy of being the child's father and of being cruel to poor Jenny. But since Allworthy refuses to listen to them, the rumors serve no ill purpose.

In Chapter X, after learning of Allworthy's fine generosity with his food, his home, and his time, we also learn that a Dr. Blifil, unsuccessful in his profession because his father forced him into it, is currently the recipient of Allworthy's generosities. The doctor, it is noted, is extremely religious, or at least has "a great appearance" of religion. He becomes increasingly fond of Miss Bridget's company and Mr. Allworthy's possessions but, being already married, cannot avail himself permanently of either. So he calls on his bachelor brother, Captain Blifil, to take advantage of both Miss Bridget's disposal to matrimony and Allworthy's declaration that since he has no other family, his sister's children will inherit his estate. The courtship between Bridget, arduously desiring a husband, and Captain Blifil, wanting the conveniences of wealth, takes less than a month. However, as soon as the marriage is accomplished and Squire Allworthy has expressed his satisfaction with the match, the captain begins to act quite coldly toward his brother who was of such great assistance. There is soon open hostility between the two men, and Allworthy speaks with the captain, stating his hatred for an unforgiving nature. The captain then appears to reconcile himself to his brother, but in private he continues to abuse him. Finally, the doctor can take it no longer and, professing a business engagement, leaves. He goes to London, where he dies soon after of "a broken heart."

Commentary

In Book I, Fielding sets the main elements of the plot in motion. We are introduced to three main characters—the squire, Miss Bridget, and the foundling, Tom Jones, though we scarcely see the infant. Fielding also provides several concealed hints about Tom's real mother: examine carefully the passages describing Miss Bridget's reactions to the child. Fielding will continue to provide this kind of dramatic foreshadowing throughout the novel, so that when we learn who Tom's parents are, it is not exactly a surprise.

Equally important, we are introduced to the main techniques of Fielding's complex and subtle style and are oriented to one of the book's major considerations, pretentiousness and hypocrisy. According to Fielding, these are two supreme evils.

The student should also be aware that a good appreciation of Fielding's novel, as with any fine work of art, requires effort. Further, Fielding explicitly indicates the kinds of subtleties that he will be using. He does this in Chapter VI with his description of Mrs. Deborah Wilkins; a close examination of that passage is warranted.

> Mrs. Deborah, having disposed of the child according to the will of her master, now prepared to visit those habitations which were supposed to conceal its mother. Not otherwise than when a kite, tremendous bird, is beheld by the feathered generation soaring aloft, and hovering over their heads, the amorous dove, and every innocent little bird, spread wide the alarm, and fly trembling to their hiding-places. . . . It is my intention, therefore, to signify, that, as it is the nature of a kite to devour little birds, so it is the nature of such persons as Mrs. Wilkins to insult and tyrannise over little people. This being indeed the means which they use to recompense to themselves their extreme servility and condescension to their superiors; for nothing can be more reasonable, than that slaves and flatterers should exact the same taxes on all below them which they themselves pay to all above them.

The kind of moral lecture which Fielding provides should be noted, for the simile and explanation are equally applicable to Captain Blifil's treatment of his brother after the marriage. Fielding uses other equally moral techniques in characterization. For example, both Miss Bridget and Mrs. Wilkins are constantly declaiming beautiful women in favor of plain and honest women. But they do this because they themselves are plain. But we learn later that they are *not* honest; they both listen at Squire Allworthy's door. Bridget, furthermore, when seeming to agree with her brother's actions, denounces them behind his back; Mrs. Wilkins never has an honest reaction because she gauges all her words and deeds on the reactions of the squire and Miss Bridget. Similarly, Doctor and Captain Blifil are hypocrites. Fielding hints (a technique he uses over and over) at Dr. Blifil's insincerity by refusing to state whether his religion is sincere. This, of course, immediately makes the reader question all of Dr. Blifil's motives, which, we soon learn, are not at all altruistic.

Another technique which Fielding uses to unveil pretense is to undercut, through indirect statement, phrases which are seemingly positive. The result is that the final, overall statement is totally negative. The best example of this occurs in Chapter XI, when the narrator is discussing Captain Blifil. After dismissing childish, immature love as capricious because it is obsessed with such external things as physical beauty, Fielding then speaks of Captain Blifil's attachment to Bridget: "The captain likewise very wisely preferred the more solid enjoyments he expected with this lady, to the fleeting charms of person. He was one of those wise men who regard beauty in the other sex as a very worthless and superficial qualification. . . ." This seems to be a laudable sentiment because it supports the ethic which the narrator has been advancing. But the next lines reverse our understanding of this seeming praise: ". . . or to speak more truly, [those] who rather choose to possess every convenience of life with an ugly woman, than a handsome one without any of these conveniences." After making a moral statement, Fielding lowers his censure with an irreversible statement of condemnation: the captain has grown so fond of Bridget's "flattering symptoms," that is, her brother's estate, "that he would most probably have contracted marriage with them, had he been obliged to have taken the witch of Endor into the bargain." This is but another way of saying that he would sell his soul for material gain. We are not through with this couple yet, for the ultimate condemnation comes, ironically, from Mr. Allworthy himself in Chapter XII. Thus one word of caution: do not consider a topic finished simply because it is no longer the immediate subject of the novel; look for the exquisitely planned moral lectures which are interrelated throughout.

There is one final technique which we should examine, that of ironic juxtaposition. In Book I we have two instances of a person's acting as a judge: Deborah Wilkins in Chapter VI and Squire Allworthy in Chapter VII. When Jenny Jones is called before Mrs. Wilkins, the narrator says, ". . . putting on the gravity of a judge, with somewhat more than his austerity, [she] began an oration with the words, 'You audacious strumpet!' in which she proceeded rather to pass sentence on the prisoner than to accuse her." Mrs. Wilkins, in her priggish and pompously assumed role, is quite an effective contrast to Allworthy, who is in fact a magistrate, but, in dealing with Jenny, shows infinite mercy, gentleness, and compassion. Indeed, his judgment is exactly that of Christ, who, when the adulteress was brought before him, said "Go, and sin no more." Christ's advice echoes Allworthy's: "Be a good girl the rest of your days." What this juxtaposition does is to emphasize that Mrs. Wilkins lacks exactly that quality which Allworthy praised in Jenny Jones: her humanity.

This first section of the novel sets up the moral situation which will continue throughout the novel: Squire Allworthy, the example of all that is good, surrounded by self-seeking, scheming pretenders to virtue. It is part of Allworthy's benevolent nature that he cannot always discern the real and the counterfeit, as in the case of Captain Blifil. This one failing in an otherwise perfect man will obviously have dire consequences.

BOOK II

Summary

Eight months after Bridget and the captain are married, they become the parents of a son. The birth of this "true heir," however, in no way detracts from Squire Allworthy's affection for his adopted foundling, though Captain Blifil spends much effort trying to convince him that bastards, due to their ignominious birth, "at the best, ought to be brought up to the lowest and vilest offices of the commonwealth." Bridget seems to agree with Blifil, for although she professes to assent to Allworthy's proposal to raise the boys together and though she is openly most kind to Tom, she privately criticizes Tom and also Allworthy's affections for him. Meanwhile, Mrs. Wilkins has not been inactive; she has managed to discover Tom's true father: the schoolmaster, Partridge.

Mrs. Partridge is as jealous as she is domineering; her naturally irritable disposition, therefore, has been even further aroused by the fact that though she has been married for nine years, she and her husband are still childless. She makes it a practice to hire only the homeliest of girls as household servants, into which category Jenny Jones fits admirably. Jenny's compensating trait, however, is intelligence. Mr. Partridge instructs her and she soon becomes a more proficient scholar than he, who, in actuality, is more convivial than he is bright. This situation leads to an unfortunate incident. At dinner one evening, Mr. Partridge says to Jenny, *"Da mihi aliquid potum."* The poor Latin causes Jenny to smile and, catching the eye of Mrs. Partridge, she blushes because she smiled at her teacher's ineptness. Mrs. Partridge, not understanding Latin, misinterprets the blush, flies into a rage, picks up a knife, and pursues Jenny, who is, fortunately, near the door. This, needless to say, marks the end of Jenny's employment there, at which Partridge is not too displeased since he has been rather annoyed by the fact that Jenny's Latin is now better than his.

For a while after Jenny's dismissal, there is relative happiness in the Partridge home. One day, however, Mrs. Partridge hears some gossip that Jenny Jones has been delivered of two bastards. Mrs. Partridge immediately concludes that her husband has been Jenny's lover. She rushes home and begins to beat, bite, and claw her unsuspecting husband. Her passions finally spent, she subsides into a screaming fit. Partridge, uncertain as to what to do, calls the neighbors for help. They arrive and, seeing Mrs. Partridge's disheveled clothes and bloody face (though the blood is her husband's), begin to berate Partridge for beating his wife.

Not surprisingly, Mrs. Wilkins soon hears of this battle and its cause. Realizing that Captain Blifil will probably succeed Mr. Allworthy as master of the estate and realizing that he has no love at all for young Tom, she informs Blifil of the story. The captain, however, admonishes her for gossiping and for her disloyalty to Allworthy. His reason for doing so is that he hopes Allworthy will hear of the matter from another source. Since this does not happen, however, Blifil takes the opportunity of a conversation on Christian charity to repeat the story to Allworthy.

Allworthy is indeed astonished and sends Mrs. Wilkins out to learn the facts. She confirms the story. Allworthy then sets a trial. Partridge pleads not guilty, but his wife testifies against him, saying that he has confessed to having an affair with Jenny. Partridge pleads innocent, declaring he made the confession only to gain a bit of peace; he says that he "would have confessed a murder from the same motive." Mrs. Partridge then breaks into tears, declaring that this is but one of her husband's many lies and accuses him of drunkenness and lechery, concluding with the statement that she herself found him and Jenny abed together. After hearing Partridge's final plea of innocence, Allworthy's only recourse is to send for Jenny. Unfortunately, she has just departed her lodgings with a recruiting officer. Allworthy then declares that testimony from such a "slut" would be of little value anyway and that, judging from the testimony of his wife, Partridge is indeed guilty. Allworthy punishes Partridge by discontinuing his annuity. So Partridge abandons himself to despair, he loses his school, and he and his wife are reduced to poverty. At length, Mrs. Partridge dies of smallpox and the schoolmaster leaves for greener fields.

In spite of all, Allworthy's affections for Tom grow. Accordingly, Captain Blifil's distaste for the child grows also, for he sees every penny spent on Tom as a decrease in his own wealth. In addition, Bridget and Blifil have begun to quarrel, often simply because they refuse on principle to agree with each other. Thus, because the captain despises the little foundling, his wife begins to caress it as though it were her own child. An event occurs, however, which restores the captain to Bridget's affections: one day, while musing over his plans for the estate when it becomes his, the captain dies of apoplexy. Bridget immediately falls into a swoon, but once a "decent time of sickness and immoderate grief" has passed, she recovers. Allworthy erects a monument bearing testimony to Blifil's charity, tenderness, sincerity, piety, and husbandly virtues.

Commentary

Book II is largely a continuation of the first book, because we are still in the introductory stages of the novel. With the conclusion of this book, all the major elements of the plot have been set in operation. The question of Tom's parentage is further developed and apparently settled. The characterization of Allworthy is also developed in a rather significant manner. The case of Partridge serves, among other things, as a prime instance of Allworthy's fallibility. He convicts Partridge of adultery on evidence he hears from highly questionable sources. In this case, Allworthy's sense of morals leads him to a too-hasty decision. As is true in a later and equally unfortunate decision, his prime error is to consider his sources of information totally reliable. Though he is a good theorist and a sincerely charitable man, he is not a sound judge of character. He has a tendency to read goodness into people's motives when goodness is not there; he judges people on the basis of his own altruistic nature. The description of his reactions to Blifil is a prime and significant example of this.

Significantly, too, Fielding continues to intensify his concentration on hypocrisy. Indeed, the only characters free from it seem to be Allworthy and the two infants. In this section of the novel, we learn of Miss Bridget's dissimulation; although she has cried out against lechery and praised chastity, we know now that her relationship with Blifil before they were married was not altogether Platonic. In fact, if one engages in the sport of counting months, he is led to the conclusion that she went to bed with Captain Blifil soon after his arrival. Also, there is Mrs. Wilkin's game of deception, one which she plays in order to be on everyone's good side — in other words, she plays both ends against the middle. Even the doctors, in an exquisitely written scene, play a "game" for a nice fee. The general public serves Fielding well; they consistently criticize everyone else, though they fail to see their own faults. At the end of Chapter VI, Fielding is deftly ironic when he writes that the townspeople accomplish one of their typical reversals of opinion; after having condemned Partridge, they begin to pity him. But nonetheless he is "in danger of starving with the universal compassion of his neighbours."

As pointed out earlier in discussing Book I, the events in Tom Jones are carefully organized; each one is not a unit in itself but often has a significant relationship to several others. The story of the Partridges is a case in point; it relates directly to the major misfortune in the book, All-worthy's rejection of Tom. The sole cause of the Partridge affair is Mrs. Partridge's jealousy which magnifies events and makes her perjure herself in Allworthy's court. Jealousy causes a dissociation from reality. The parallel being gradually worked out here is Bridget's jealous guarding of Tom's fortune, which causes Squire Allworthy, Captain Blifil, and even Mrs. Wilkins to show favoritism to young Blifil.

Another matter which appears in Book II and will become important later concerns the death of the "villains" in this section of the novel, Captain Blifil and Mrs. Partridge. Both of these characters are representative of what has been described as one of the major evils with which the novel is concerned, self-seeking pretenders to virtue. Captain Blifil's greed for the Allworthy estate, the narrator implies, causes his apoplexy, a rupture of a blood vessel. "Just at the very instant when his heart was exulting in meditations on the happiness which would accrue to him by Mr. Allworthy's death, he himself—died of an apoplexy." Mrs. Partridge's jealousy leads her to lie about her husband, who is then convicted and punished because of those lies. This, in turn, results in their being reduced to dire poverty, and Mrs. Partridge soon dies of smallpox. In both cases, poetic justice reigns. This is one of the ways in which a comedy remains comic. When an artist is portraying human weaknesses, if he allows those weaknesses to dominate, he has a tragedy, or at least something other than comedy. That is, if Captain Blifil were allowed to succeed Allworthy, Tom Jones might possibly begin to read like Dicken's Oliver Twist.

The conclusion of Book II compels us to examine Fielding's principles of selection. Obviously, everything which appears in any work of art is there because the artist chooses to include it in order to achieve some particular purpose. When an author goes to the effort to portray fully some of his characters, as Fielding does with the brothers Blifil and Mrs. Partridge, only to kill them off a few pages later, we must certainly ask what his purpose is. If it is only to advance the plot, which these characters do, then full characterization is rather superfluous. Further, if we also assume that the characters serve more than just to exhibit the artist's abilities, then we must look at them as "thematic characters." With this in mind, it seems that a careful examination of Book II will assuredly support the view that Captain Blifil and Mrs. Partridge serve more to help Fielding establish a moral viewpoint than they do any other purpose. The importance which these characters serve in revealing to the reader the importance which the narrator attaches to jealousy and egocentricity has been discussed.

Fielding also uses the captain to satirize ethical Christian charity against which all other actions are to be judged. He does this with one of his masterful touches of irony, for Blifil, pursuing his attempt to remove Tom from Allworthy's affections, slyly discloses the tale concerning Partridge and Jenny during a discussion of the meaning of charity in the Bible. Blifil states that the word denotes "candour, or the forming of a benevolent opinion of our brethren, and passing a favourable judgment on their actions." This is, of course, precisely what Blifil is *not* doing to poor Partridge. Conversely, it is exactly what Allworthy is constantly attempting to do; we are given the example of his "charity" to Blifil as an example. Furthermore, Blifil also states that charity does not mean giving money to the poor. In fact, he says, giving money to the impoverished harms them more than it helps. He cites scriptural references to support his point, but naturally neglects to cite such passages as that concerning the widow who gives her last penny to the poor. Since Fielding has characterized Blifil so fully, we realize that Blifil is again rationalizing his own niggardly egotism. Like the examples of the effects of jealousy, this lesson in spiritual benevolence is extremely important, for as Allworthy fails in judging Partridge, he will later fail to be charitable in judging Tom.

BOOK III

Summary

The narrator reintroduces us to Tom Jones, now about fourteen years old, a young man who, it seems, is rather prone to vice. At least, everyone in Allworthy's home has long proclaimed this to be the case and wondered why Allworthy allows Tom to remain in the same house with young Blifil, who is as virtuous as Tom is dishonest. Tom is particularly prone to robbery and has been convicted of three such crimes: stealing fruit from an orchard, a duck from a farmyard, and a ball from young Blifil's pocket. However, it is generally unknown that the first two of these were done for the needy family of Allworthy's gamekeeper.

The narrator cites a further example of Tom's "malevolence." One day Tom and the gamekeeper were hunting and flushed a covey of partridges, which flew into Squire Western's game preserve. Tom persuaded the gamekeeper to pursue them and they soon managed to shoot one of the birds. The owner, who was nearby, rode up to them and, discovering Tom with the bird (the gamekeeper had hidden in a thicket), went immediately to report this to Allworthy. Allworthy severely admonished Tom and demanded to know who had been with him. Knowing this could cause the gamekeeper to lose his job, Tom refused to tell. Allworthy turned Tom over to Mr. Thwackum, the clergyman who had been employed to tutor Tom and Blifil. Thwackum was equally unsuccessful in discovering Tom's partner in mischief and gave Tom a sound whipping. Allworthy, who abhorred cruelty and injustice, decided the punishment had been too harsh. He apologized to Tom and, to make amends, gave him a little horse. Tom was sincerely overcome by Allworthy's goodness. Thwackum, however, was convinced that Tom was still in the lap of evil and needed another whipping. Fortunately for Tom, Thwackum's words prompted a response from Mr. Square, the boys' other tutor. The two learned men were soon engulfed in one of their frequent heated debates.

Just at this moment, a rather more physical debate breaks out between the two boys: Blifil calls Tom "a beggarly bastard." Blifil, who receives a bloody nose in the scuffle, denies this and, to support his denial, informs Allworthy that it was Black George, the gamekeeper, who was shooting partridges with Tom. Thwackum, enraged, is prepared to pounce on Tom, but Allworthy, having more patience, asks Tom why he refused to tell. Tom then relates the whole story, affirming that Black George had gone into the preserve, but only at Tom's bidding and even then reluctantly. Tom begs Allworthy to be merciful to George and his family, saying "Do, pray, sir, let me be punished; take my little horse away again; but pray, sir, forgive poor George." Allworthy dismisses the boys and later, in private, states that he thinks that Tom deserves reward rather than punishment. Thwackum, "whose meditations [are] full of birch," thinks the opposite true, citing texts to prove it. Square, for reasons of his own, agrees with Thwackum. They also agree in praising Master Blifil. Though Allworthy does not punish Tom, he does dismiss Black George.

Square and Thwackum much prefer Master Blifil over Tom. Blifil is diligent in his lessons, memorizes the favorite phrases of both gentlemen, and caters to their every wish: "With one he was all religion, with the other he was all virtue...when both were present, he was profoundly silent, which both interpreted in his favor." Tom is not so self-effacing, "often forgetting to pull off his hat or to bow at his master's approach," and sometimes he even expressed a bit of skepticism about the beliefs of his tutors. More important, however, is the fact that both men desire to marry Blifil's mother. They think that showing preference to her son is the surest way to her heart. Their motive is the same as the late Captain Blifil's: Allworthy's estate. Both men are able to square this desire with their philosophies.

Widow Blifil is indeed aware of the two men's goals and, although she has no intention of marrying again, she is pleased with the flattering attention she receives from them; "she was rather inclined to favor the parson's principles; but Square's person was more agreeable to her, for he was a comely man."

Actually, both tutors are wrong in their appraisal of the widow. The distasteful memory of her husband makes her hate her son and prefer Tom. By the time Tom is eighteen, Bridget's favoritism is quite obvious, and the whole countryside begins to whisper about her love for the boy, believing "he has become a rival to both Square and Thwackum." As a result, Allworthy begins to show preference for Blifil.

One day Thwackum discovers that Tom has sold the horse which Allworthy gave him. He asks the reason but Tom refuses to tell him. Only Allworthy's appearance saves Tom from another beating. Upon asking Tom privately, Allworthy discovers that Tom sold the horse in order to give the money to Black George, whose family is starving and nearly naked. Allworthy, of course, forgives Tom. Not much later, Tom, for the same reason, sells his Bible, also a gift from Allworthy. When this is discovered, a repetition of the questioning takes place.

Allworthy, as a result of Tom's actions, intends to rehire Black George, but when he learns that George killed a rabbit on Squire Western's manor, he decides against it. It is Master Blifil, inordinately fond of justice, who brings this crime to Allworthy's attention. Blifil also slightly exaggerates the crime, but Allworthy never discovers this.

Tom, who has become great friends with Squire Western, due to his equestrian and hunting skills, now decides to prevail upon him, through his daughter Sophia, to hire Black George—no easy undertaking since George has, by means of the rabbit incident, made himself most unpopular.

Commentary

Fielding's major undertaking in Book III is to provide us with an understanding of the two young men in the Allworthy home, Master Blifil and Tom Jones. They are exact opposites. Tom, as evidenced by his active concern for Black George, is basically sympathetic, generous, and kind. He has, in other words, some of Allworthy's best qualities. Tom is also honest. He never lies to escape punishment or to gain an advantage for himself. On the other hand, Blifil always acts in accordance with carefully planned schemes to advance his own interests. Not once do we see Blifil thinking of anyone but himself. In his education, he learns what he thinks will please his tutors. When he praises someone, he does so in order that he himself will be better thought of. What is worse, he is totally unscrupulous: he lies, he schemes, and he breaks confidences. And it is someone like Tom or George who usually suffers. But at least we know that he came by these traits honestly, his father, Captain Blifil, played the same game. The difference between the two boys can be stated quite succinctly: Tom sincerely loves Allworthy and cares for others; Blifil loves only himself.

A second important feature in Book III is that Allworthy's "blindness" to much that goes on around him is again emphasized. Allworthy seemingly cannot judge motives. He does not see, for example, that Square and Thwackum are competing to marry Bridget and inherit the estate. He does not recognize Master Blifil's character. When the narrator presents us with as many examples as he does here of Allworthy's misunderstanding, what was earlier seen as a minor fault becomes a glaring error. We can now see the importance of the narrator's repeated concern in Book II with "overlooking flaws in an otherwise good character." He is posing a moral question for us, and the question directly concerns one of the most benevolent men in England, Squire Allworthy: how much can we safely overlook? Are we not gradually being forced to alter our high opinion of Allworthy?

Further, Allworthy's concern with total justice and equity leads him into other difficulties. When he perceives his sister's preferential treatment of Tom over Blifil, he, to counteract any effects this might have, begins to show more love for Blifil than for Tom. Surely Allworthy should be able to see that this would create far more problems than it would solve. This is the kind of reasoning which considers abstracts in a vacuum, the kind of logic that reasons that if you are standing with one foot on a block of ice and one foot on a hot stove, you will be perfectly comfortable.

Finally, Book III provides us with two of the most delightfully comic characters in the novel, Square and Thwackum. It seems that Fielding is least patient with pedantic pretenders to knowledge and, just as he undermined our faith in Partridge's scholarly character, so he soon makes it impossible for us to believe Thwackum or Square capable of teaching anything but boorishness and servility. Also, it is to Fielding's credit as a novelist that Square and Thwackum are at once individualized characters and representatives of a type. Besides their characterization and the comedy they provide, they also serve to ridicule two eighteenth-century philosophies and to castigate a blind and rigidly narrow view of life. It is to the discredit of their philosophies and their integrity that Square and Thwackum can rationalize any course of action they take, from courting Miss Bridget to flogging poor Tom.

Briefly, Square is a kind of parody of Lord Shaftesbury, a prominent eighteenth-century deist-Platonist. Square, like the deist, believes that man is inherently good and will be perfectly good if he but follows his *natural* instincts, for "evil is a derivation from our nature." Thwackum is a Tory who rigidly adheres to the views of the established Church of England: "When I mention religion I mean the Christian religion; and not only the Christian religion, but the Protestant religion; and not only the Protestant religion, but the Church of England." Both men are interested in seeing that *others,* like Tom, adhere to their precepts. As for their own conduct, they do what they please.

BOOK IV

Summary

Fielding brings his heroine, Miss Sophia Western, onto the stage in the most grandiloquent manner possible. At the age of eighteen, she is a most charming lady. Her beautifully proportioned body is equalled by her intelligence, and her natural inclinations have been improved by the careful instructions of her aunt, for her mother died some time ago. An only child, she is deeply loved by her father.

Although Squires Allworthy and Western are of totally different natures, they manage to remain on friendly terms. So Blifil, Tom, and Sophia, being nearly the same age, have spent much time together from early childhood. Sophia has always preferred Tom to Blifil, and the latter, although he has never shown it, has always been resentful. One day, for instance, when the Allworthy family was dining with the Westerns and the children were playing outside, Blifil persuaded Sophia to let him hold the bird which Tom had given her and which she treasured. Blifil, venting his spite, let the bird fly away. Sophia, much distressed, began to scream. Tom, seeing the bird in a tree, tried to recapture it, but a branch broke and he tumbled into a pond. Sophia now screamed louder, bringing the adults to discover the trouble. Blifil related the story, telling them that he pitied the poor bird and, in accord with the principles of nature and religion, gave it its freedom. Both Square and Thwackum were much impressed with the effects of their teaching on Blifil. Allworthy saw good in both boys' actions, but Squire Western cursed Blifil for his cruelty to Sophia and praised Tom. Sophia, of course, could detect what Allworthy could not: Blifil's motive of revenge. The incident served to heighten her affection for Tom and her aversion to Blifil.

From that time on, Tom and Western have become close friends. Tom has frequently been invited to dine with him and, through his "natural gallantry and good nature," he has won Sophia's love. Knowing Sophia's influence with Western, Tom requests her to ask her father to give Black George a position on the manor. Sophia replies that she will do all she can. This is more than sufficient, for after she plies her father with all his favorite tunes on the harpsichord, he is willing to grant almost any wish. George is given the position.

The reason for Tom's seeming insensitivity to Sophia's charms is that he thinks himself in love with another—Molly Seagrim, the daughter of Black George. "So little had she of modesty, that Jones had more regard for her virtue than she herself." In fact, she is so clever at seducing Tom that she convinces him that he is seducing her. Molly is the object of Tom's love, "though greater beauty, or a fresher object, might have been more so." Naturally, Molly soon becomes pregnant.

To conceal her condition, Molly wears one of the lovely dresses Sophia has given her. But when she wears this dress to church, it causes her peers to act with envy, scorn, and derision. After the county's worthies have departed, a magnificent battle in the church graveyard ensues, with mud, dirt, and fruit being thrown at Molly. Molly clubs numerous women with a handy thighbone and launches a ferocious hand-to-hand (and hand-to-hair) combat between herself and Goody Brown. The battle is interrupted by the intervention of Tom Jones, who with Blifil and Square, happens to ride past the church. Tom comes to Molly's rescue and, after having dispersed the crowd with his horsewhip, he, Blifil, and Square escort Miss Seagrim home.

When Molly returns home, she is no less fiercely reviled, though in words only, for her brashness. The quarrel is ended by the entrance of Black George, who informs the family that Miss Western has offered Molly a position in her house. This, because of Molly's obvious pregnancy, causes more consternation and heated discussion—cooled only when George resorts to using a switch—and it is finally decided that Molly's older sister will apply for the job.

The next evening, Tom dines with the Westerns and Parson Supple. The parson relates the above tale, adding that a fiddler who had his head broken during the churchyard battle has brought charges against Molly. Further, while Molly was in Allworthy's court answering to the fiddler, it was discovered that she was soon to be delivered of a bastard, so Allworthy immediately assigned her to Bridewell Prison. Upon hearing this, Tom's face pales, he excuses himself, and Squire Western declares with approval, "I smoke it. Tom is certainly the father of this bastard." Sophia is most disconcerted.

Upon entering the gate to Allworthy's house, Tom sees Molly being escorted out by the constable. He halts them, embraces Molly, threatens violence to anyone who would touch her, and then tells the constable to wait while he speaks with Allworthy. Finding Allworthy, Tom confesses to being the father of Molly's child and begs him to set Molly free and lay all blame on him. Allworthy obliges him and gives Tom a severe lecture, much like the one given Jenny Jones some years ago. Thwackum, with much invective, entreats for a sterner punishment for Tom. Allworthy, however, feels the boy is sincerely penitent and will not transgress again. Thus Square tries his wily logic on Allworthy; he declares that all of Tom's generosity to Black George has been for the sole purpose of retaining Molly as his whore. Allworthy is most disquieted by this convincing reasoning.

Sophia, recovering somewhat from her initial shock, decides to be indifferent to Tom; but one meeting with him shows her that she cannot. She then decides to see as little of him as possible. But this is not to be, for one day when they are out hunting, Tom rescues Sophia from her bucking horse and breaks his arm. Needless to say, Sophia is greatly impressed. Since Tom stays at the Western manor while his arm is mending, Sophia's maid, Honour, is quick to tell her mistress of several instances when she heard Tom speak most favorably and endearingly of Sophia. Sophia is touched; Jones recaptures her heart.

Commentary

In this section of the novel, two important events occur. The first is the Seagrim affair, which basically serves to further characterize Tom. Although we believe in Tom's goodness, perhaps more than ever, we see that he tends to be caught up in the moment, giving little thought to future consequences. In a word, he is imprudent—a fault which will become even more important throughout the remainder of the novel. Also, the Seagrim incident, transformed by Square's ingenious interpretation, is a rather large step in Allworthy's continuing disenchantment with Tom.

The second important occurrence is the beginning of the love affair between Tom and Sophia. At this point, the student would do well to consider the importance of some of the names Fielding uses—such names as "Allworthy," "Thwackum," and "Square." *Sophia* is the Greek word for wisdom and Tom's gaining of "sophia" is indeed an important thematic consideration.

Furthermore, Book IV contains some of the most delightfully amusing passages in English literature. It must not be just read, but reread in order for all of its subtleties to be savored. The highlights of the book are, of course, the mock-heroic description of Sophia and the narration of the battle scene.

Before examining these scenes in more detail, it should be pointed out that once again Fielding is pairing characters for us. After the glowing description of Sophia, the spotlight is not on the beautiful heroine but on Molly Seagrim. Molly is a relatively unimportant character in herself, but she serves as a foil to Sophia. In describing Molly, Fielding says she was "one of the handsomest girls in the country"—but unfortunately, her "handsomeness" would be better suited to a man. She is another of Fielding's self-centered characters: she cares only for her own pleasure and comfort. No one could better serve to make Sophia's true goodness and beauty stand out. Also, Squire Western is, in one sense, a foil to Squire Allworthy. Western is crude, rakish, boorish, loud and lacks all of the learning and refinement that Allworthy has. But Western is refreshingly straightforward; in his honest reactions, he shows the common sense that Allworthy seemingly does not possess. It is Western, not Allworthy, who correctly sums up the incident in which Blifil frees Sophia's bird; he cannot help telling Blifil that if he were a son of his, "his backside should be well flead." Though Western's overbearing concern with material goods is perhaps not very attractive, his basic instincts are usually correct. Perhaps best of all, Western knows how to laugh — another trait which Allworthy seems to lack.

Turning to the mock-heroic scenes, examine briefly some of their major characteristics. Fielding's lengthy preface informs us of the light-hearted manner in which we are to read his introduction of Sophia: "Our intention, in short, is to introduce our heroine with the utmost solemnity in our power, with an elevation of style, and all other circumstance proper to raise the veneration of our reader." He then begins in the traditional heroic manner by calling on nature to acknowledge the beauty of the lady. After a few hyperbolic comparisons, he begins the equally traditional "anatomizing," describing Sophia's every feature most eloquently. If the description complies with the tradition, why do we call it *mock*-heroic? The answer is that we can tell by the context and by Fielding's subtle hints. To say the least, an elevated description of this kind is highly obtrusive in a comedy of manners, into which category *Tom Jones* loosely fits. Such a description is usually reserved for works with a highly serious tone and for women of great and universal importance, such as Helen of Troy. Also in this passage, there are three or four abrupt descents from the lofty sphere. The first occurs when Fielding, using personification, refers to "the sharp-pointed nose of bitter-biting Eurus" (the east wind). Then, after luxuriant descriptions and numerous comparisons in the most stately of tones, suddenly we read the quite mundane, colloquial sentence: "Sophia, then . . . was a middle-sized woman; but rather inclining to tall." The juxtaposition of the two styles humorously points up the outrageous superfluity of the epic description by recalling us to the proper level of the novel. This device works because Fielding can truly write well in the elevated style. Reread the opening paragraphs of Chapter II and note the carefully balanced, smoothly flowing sentences, the carefully placed alliteration, and the rather pronounced rhythm. The English is lovely and decorative — but hollow, exactly the effect Fielding wanted.

The mocking aspect of another passage is more obvious and perhaps more humorous. In Chapter VIII, Fielding describes Molly Seagrim's battle in the churchyard with all the stylistic devices Homer would have devoted to narrating a battle of the Trojan War. (For a better understanding of the tradition Fielding is satirizing, one should read Book III of Homer's *Iliad*.) Therein lies the reason for calling it mock-heroic: the lowliest, most insignificant incident is described with the traditional epic machinery. The epic devices used here are: the invocation to the muse of poetry to grant the poet sufficient power to complete his task; the "catalogue," or listing of the combatants, including a brief biographical sketch; the final battle between the two "heroes," Molly Seagrim and Goody Brown; and, of course, the elevated diction, set off by the mundane. For example, Fielding first describes the weapons used by Molly's attackers as "missiles" which are "dreadful to a well-dressed lady." One paragraph later he translates this as, "they pelted her with dirt and rubbish."

In addition, Fielding infuses his own brand of irony into the description. While describing Molly's vigorous opponent, Goody Brown, Fielding relates that she, "equally famous in the fields of Venus as of Mars," has cuckolded her husband innumerable times. Also, note Fielding's account of Molly's advance on her foes: "Molly then taking a thighbone in her hand, fell in among the flying ranks, and dealing her blows with great liberality on either side, overthrew the carcass of many a mighty hero and heroine." Here Fielding is drawing a parallel with Samson, the Old Testament hero who "found a new jawbone of an ass, and put forth his hand and took it, and slew a thousand men therewith" (Judges 15:15). Fielding could depend on his readers, who were thoroughly familiar with the Bible, to make the connection. The difference between the two stories is that while Samson fought for his God, Molly is defending her non-existent virtue — in which case, the thighbone is a most apt replacement for Samson's jawbone.

BOOK V

Summary

While Tom is recuperating in Squire Western's home, he has several visitors who take the opportunity of lecturing at length. Allworthy speaks repeatedly of Tom's misdoings, advising that he must mend his ways or lose his happiness and his adopted father's favor. Thwackum pronounces Tom's accident a visitation of God's wrath and is surprised that it has not occurred earlier. Square says that accidents happen to fools and wise men alike and must be borne. Blifil seldom visits Tom; when he does, he is never alone, fearing that he might be "contaminated." Squire Western is Tom's constant visitor, a pleasure increased by the fact that he often brings Sophia with him.

When Tom is somewhat better, he sits and listens to Sophia play the harpsichord for hours. Though Sophia diligently attempts to conceal her feelings, Tom notices certain signs of affection. However, Tom is not the boldest of men and thinks perhaps he is reading love into what is but kindness and concern. Besides, he knows Squire Western would never allow him to woo Sophia; though they are the best of friends, the squire has declared that he would see Sophia wedded to "one of the richest men in the country." Tom also knows that Allworthy would think his taking advantage of Western's hospitality by wooing his daughter one of the basest acts imaginable. But more weighty than these considerations is Tom's compassion for Molly, who, he is certain, would be utterly lost should he desert her. "His own heart would not suffer him to destroy a human creature who, he thought, loved him, and had to that love sacrificed her innocence." So Tom is determined to forget Sophia.

Mrs. Honour, Sophia's maid, is also one of Tom's frequent visitors. On one particular occasion, she tells Tom that she has informed Sophia that she saw Tom kissing one of her mistress' muffs; as a consequence, Sophia has now developed a deep fondness for that particular muff. Honour's story is broken short by the arrival of Western, who takes Tom downstairs to hear Sophia play the harpsichord. Tom immediately notices that Sophia is wearing the muff in question. While she is playing the squire's favorite tune, the muff slips down her arm, causing her to miss several notes. Western, in a fit of pique, throws the muff into the fire, but Sophia immediately recovers it. The narrator remarks that men are frequently most impressed by the tiniest of events, and that "the citadel of Jones was taken by surprise. All those considerations of honour and prudence which our hero had lately with so much military wisdom placed as guards over the avenue of his heart ran away from their posts, and the God of Love marched in, in triumph."

Nonetheless, Tom is still greatly concerned about what will happen to Molly. After much fretting, he decides to offer her some money, for since he cannot make her happy by his presence, perhaps he can console her by easing her poverty. Accordingly, he visits her home. Her mother says that Molly is out, but a sister tells Tom, "with a malicious smile," that Molly is in bed. Tom mounts the stairs, but the door is barred, and he is not let in for some time because, as Molly explains, she was asleep. Molly, no doubt because of her joy at seeing Tom, is flustered. Tom is so impressed with this that, for a while, he forgets the purpose of his visit. But "after the first transports of their meeting [are] over," he broaches the subject. Molly bursts into tears and upbraids him for his unforgivable falseness, saying, "I can never love any other man as long as I live."

Molly's protestations are interrupted and her case quite refuted by the precipitous fall of the closet curtain. The entire contents of the closet are revealed and ". . . among other female utensils appeared (with shame I write it, and with sorrow will it be read) — the philosopher Square, in a posture (for the place would not near admit his standing upright) as ridiculous as can possibly be imagined." Whereupon the narrator remarks that although philosophers think more wisely than others, "they always act exactly like other men."

Being the first to recover from his astonishment, Tom breaks into fits of laughter and proceeds to help Square from his uncomfortable position, stating that he has no desire to expose Square's behavior and has, in fact, never been better pleased with his activities. Tom leaves after he has counselled Square to treat Molly kindly. He later discovers from Molly's sister that Will Barnes, and not Tom, was the first to seduce Molly and is, in all probability, the father of her child. This leaves Tom's heart free to be possessed entirely by Sophia.

Tom, in spite of the fact that his arm has healed, continues to stay with the Westerns, for the squire greatly enjoys his company and Tom is easily persuaded to stay. During this time, Tom and Sophia become increasingly aware of their love for each other, although Tom is still troubled by thoughts of Squire Western's and Squire Allworthy's reactions.

During Tom's absence from his home, Allworthy becomes quite ill with a fever. Indeed, the doctor gives him up as lost, and Allworthy settles all his worldly affairs and calls his family around his bed to inform them of his will. Except for annuities to Tom and Mrs. Bridget and rather generous gifts to Thwackum and Square, Allworthy leaves his entire estate to Blifil. Upon hearing Allworthy's bequest to him, Tom is emotionally overwhelmed and speaks of his love and gratitude to Allworthy, ending with the simple but eloquent cry, "O, my friend, my father!" Allworthy replies, "I am convinced, my child, that you have much goodness, generosity, and honour, in your temper: if you will add prudence and religion to these, you must be happy; for the three former qualities, I admit, make you worthy of happiness, but they are the latter only which will put you in possession of it." At this point, an attorney from Salisbury arrives with an urgent message for Allworthy, which the feverish squire sends Blifil to receive. The rest begin to leave the bedside and, once outside Allworthy's room, Thwackum, Square, and Mrs. Wilkins complain bitterly of Allworthy's small gifts to them.

Mr. Blifil returns with the news that his mother has died of gout on the road home from Salisbury. After some debate, Blifil decides he must tell Allworthy, for he would never think of keeping anything secret from him. When they arrive at his room, they find Allworthy already much recovered. So Blifil, discreetly tearful, informs Allworthy of the news.

That evening, the doctor says that Allworthy is out of danger. Tom, who had hitherto been quite dejected, is suddenly overjoyed and proceeds to indulge himself in a bout of heavy drinking in celebration of Allworthy's recovery. Blifil, however, is offended by Tom's gaiety. Tom replies that in his happiness he had simply forgotten about Blifil's dead mother. A quarrel and scuffle ensue and are quelled only by Thwackum's intervention.

Tom then goes for a walk and, with thoughts of Sophia and the delicious smells of the ripening summer, he becomes hopelessly submerged in thoughts of love. While Tom is thus enraptured, Molly Seagrim passes by on her way home. After a few moments of discussing their last encounter, they retire into a nearby thicket.

As it happens, Blifil and Thwackum pass by and see Molly and Tom disappear into the grove. They pursue the couple, but make so much noise that they find only Tom. Thwackum demands to know what "slut" Tom has been with. Tom refuses to tell and a battle begins, with Tom fighting both Blifil and Thwackum. After a few minutes, however, a passerby, noting the unfair odds, intercedes and soon he and Tom are victorious. The helper is none other than Squire Western.

Soon the rest of the Western party rides up, and Sophia, seeing Tom splotched with blood, faints. Amid the confusion, Tom takes Sophia to a nearby stream, splashes water on her, and she revives. Squire Western is joyous and reaffirms his undying love for Tom. After the squire discovers the reason for the battle and searches about for the girl, much as he would for a fox, Sophia declares she fears a relapse is coming on. So they depart with Tom accompanying them, leaving Thwackum and Blifil to nurse their wounded pride.

Commentary

Fielding, with unflagging industry, continues to unveil hypocrisy. Not only is Square revealed to be subject to the all-too-human vice of lust, but he, Thwackum, and Deborah Wilkins are shown for what they are. When we see them complaining about Allworthy's will, we discover the true motives for their seemingly selfless actions.

Book V is also important in setting the stage for further developments concerning the two prime factors in Tom's life — Allworthy's favor and Sophia's love. In fact, the pattern is firmly established, for Tom is *almost* successful, only to spoil his success by a rash action. For example, as soon as Sophia has recovered from learning that Tom has been Molly's lover, she discovers him in the thicket fighting because of the wench. Similarly, when Tom has regained Allworthy's favor, he gets drunk and commits the same sin of lechery and also battles Blifil and Thwackum; it is, in fact, this very event which will be Tom's downfall. Concerning this, Squire Allworthy's "last words" to Tom are important here. It is Tom's imprudence or rashness which will bring about his downfall. Allworthy is stating that Tom must not only *be* good, he must also *appear* to be good; he must be discreet. This is but another way of saying that appearances are as important as truth — surely a lesson Tom could easily have learned simply by watching any of the several masters of hypocrisy around him.

BOOK VI

Summary

Squire Western's sister, whom we have but briefly seen, is a woman of learning. She reads widely — political pamphlets, contemporary drama, poetry, and classical literature. She has also spent much time in London and at court, and considers herself knowledgeable about affairs of state. She also considers herself an authority on love, although her knowledge is all theoretical since she has had no direct experience, being rather formidable to men — both in size (over six feet tall) and scholarship. This "knowledgeable" lady detects what she thinks are the signs of love in Sophia's conduct and, after carefully observing Sophia for two weeks, she is absolutely certain. She announces this to the squire, who rages at his daughter's audacity in not consulting him, claiming that "if she marries the man I would have her, she may love whom she pleases." His sister informs him that he has no need to worry, for Sophia is in love with none other than Mr. Blifil. The squire is indeed happy; he has long contemplated the results of combining his and Allworthy's estates. Upon advice from his sister, Western decides to propose the match to Allworthy.

The chance to make the proposal presents itself soon when the Allworthy family dines with the Westerns. But a complication develops: Mrs. Western, on the preceding day, has hinted so much to Sophia that Sophia thinks her love for Tom has been found out. So, during dinner, she ignores Tom and lavishes her attention upon young Mr. Blifil. The squire takes this as a good omen and approaches Allworthy concerning the marriage. Allworthy states that he is most pleased and hopes that the young people's affections lead that way. Western is disappointed with this response; he has always felt that "parents [are] the best judges of proper matches for their children."

Nevertheless, as soon as they return home, Allworthy informs Blifil of the proposal. Blifil, though neither charmed by Sophia nor a man of great passion, does lust after material gain and has often thought of possessing the Western estate. Thus he tells Allworthy that he has not much thought of matrimony, but would defer to his uncle's wishes in all things. Blifil then launches into such a discourse on love and marriage that Allworthy feels Blifil has that regard for Sophia "which in sober and virtuous minds is the sure foundation of friendship and love." Allworthy then writes a letter of confirmation to Western, who is so pleased that, without consulting Sophia, he sets a date for the courtship to begin.

Mrs. Western, at her brother's urging, goes to Sophia's room to inform her of her impending happiness. During the conversation, however, Mrs. Western learns that it is Tom whom Sophia loves and that she detests Blifil. Mrs. Western flies into a rage and berates Sophia for her lack of breeding in condescending to love a bastard; "can the blood of the Westerns submit to such contamination?" The two ladies finally compromise: if Sophia will entertain Blifil, Mrs. Western will not inform the squire of Sophia's misplaced affections.

When Sophia and Blifil are alone that afternoon, there is a fifteen-minute silence, followed by a sudden burst of Blifil's compliments, which Sophia receives with monosyllabic responses and lowered head. After a few more minutes, Sophia departs. Blifil, being totally inexperienced, thinks this normal and is quite happy. When leaving, he tells the squire of his conquest. Western, overjoyed, finds Sophia and begins to pour out his abundance of parental love for her, stating that his happiness is totally dependent on hers. Sophia takes this opportunity to tell her father that he could make her infinitely happy by *not* forcing her to marry Blifil. At this, Squire Western becomes enraged and shouts, "I am resolved upon the match, and unless you consent to it I will not give you a groat . . . though I saw you expiring with famine in the street, I would not relieve you with a morsel of bread." As the squire storms out of the room, he meets Tom and, with much swearing, tells him of his daughter's ungrateful turn of mind. Tom, who knows nothing of the matter, says that he will speak to Sophia and try to get her to agree to the match.

Tom, of course, after a few endearing words of comfort, asks Sophia to do exactly the opposite — to promise that she will never marry Blifil.

Sophia replies, "Be assured I never will give him what is in my power to withhold from him."

While the two lovers are talking, Mrs. Western, upon learning of Sophia's request of her father, tells the squire of Sophia's love for Tom. Western then, as on other occasions, responds with fury, vowing the destruction of Jones. It is only by Parson Supple's physical intervention that the squire is stopped from attacking poor Tom. After Tom leaves, Western declares that he will inform Allworthy of Tom's unforgivable actions.

Western does indeed inform Allworthy and requests him to kindly keep the rascal away from his house. After Western leaves, Blifil, for whom "the success of Jones was much more grievous than the loss of Sophia," acquaints Allworthy of the events on the day the will was read — of Tom's "drunkenness and debauchery," of his meeting with Molly, and of the attack on Thwackum and himself. Blifil has carefully saved this tale, which he alters to suit his purposes, for just such a time as this. Allworthy sends for Thwackum who corroborates every detail of Blifil's story.

That evening after dinner, Allworthy confronts Tom, telling him that unless he can clear himself of Blifil's charges, he will be banished forever. Jones, already despairing because of Sophia, can say nothing in rebuttal. So Allworthy commands him to leave the house immediately and gives him 500 pounds. The neighbors, who had once unanimously censored Allworthy for rearing Tom, now unanimously censor him for this cruelty.

After leaving the house, Tom walks less than a mile and throws himself down by a brook and falls into a fit of despair. He recovers and proceeds to a house to write a letter to Sophia. There, he discovers that while bemoaning his fate, he lost his wallet containing the money Allworthy gave him. On his way back to look for the money, Tom meets Black George who offers to help him search. They do not find the money, however, for Black George, who passed by earlier, has it safely in his pocket.

Meanwhile, we learn that Squire Western has virtually imprisoned his daughter in her room, setting Mrs. Honour as her guard. But although Western has forbidden such things, Honour does deliver Tom's letter to Sophia, who, upon reading it, bursts into tears of despair. She decides to send Tom all the money she has — sixteen guineas. Honour gives it to Black George to deliver. After debating whether to keep it, George is goaded by fear of being discovered into taking the money to Tom.

Commentary

With the conclusion of Book VI, the first third of the novel, Tom has apparently lost all he ever gained—Allworthy's love, blessings, and generosity, and the chance to be with Sophia. With this book, too, we make the transition from the country to the road and the beginning of the picaresque section of the novel. Appropriately, Fielding manages to warn us of what Tom has in store for him en route to the city. Considering the city, note the character of Mrs. Western; Fielding takes every opportunity to prejudice us against her kind of "city" education. The narrator constantly speaks of that kind of learning in connection with deceit, foppery, innuendo, and other affectations which one uses to cover his true feelings. One immediately realizes, and this is one of the ironies in the novel, that Mr. Blifil has learned all of these lessons perfectly without once venturing into the city. Nevertheless, the kind of people one must deal with in the city are much more insidious and the quality of life suffers immensely. It is not a question of being virtuous in the city, for that is nearly impossible; it is rather a question of constantly fending off as much evil as one can recognize. Much of it is cleverly disguised.

One of the important literary analogues to *Tom Jones* is that of the fall from innocence to the knowledge of good and evil—the story of the Garden of Eden. Book VI presents us with the equivalent of God's casting Adam and Eve out of the garden because of their disobedience: Tom is banished from Allworthy's home. Tom is moving from a relatively protected existence at Allworthy's estate into the threatening world outside. To gain a better idea of how Eden-like Allworthy's home is, we should reread the description of the estate in Book I, Chapter IV; a more perfect, harmonious setting would be hard to imagine. Further, it is significant that early in Book VII, Fielding inserts an allusion to Milton's *Paradise Lost.*

> And now having taken a resolution to leave the country, [Tom] began to debate with himself whither he should go. The world, as Milton phrases it, lay all before him; and Jones, no more than Adam, had any man to whom he might resort for comfort or assistance.

A final remark concerning Book VI is that Fielding is making a rather important point concerning priorities. In the third chapter

Fielding remarks that a good general rule of conduct is "don't buy at too dear a price." This is particularly applicable to Squire Western who is intent on merging his and Allworthy's estates. His uppermost motive concerning Sophia's wedding is monetary gain. (We have seen the trait before in Captain Blifil, Square, Thwackum, and even Mr. Blifil.) The squire wants to "buy" the estate at the expense of his daughter's happiness; and not only does Sophia detest Blifil, but, as we know, Blifil is indeed a poor friend and companion. Western himself has expressed his displeasure with Blifil before, but is willing, even eager, to overlook his earlier assessment in order to see his coffers expanded. He is, in fact, so bent on this pairing that he actually does physical violence to his beloved daughter. Though Western is usually a comic figure — because of the extremes in his nature — he becomes almost despicable simply because of his powerful will to dominate. He is, however, partially redeemed by his basic generosity. It is, again, a question of how much one is willing to overlook.

On the other hand, the squire's sister is a totally comic figure; her worst fault is her pretension to wisdom. Unfortunately, her theoretical knowledge, as in the case of judging Sophia's love, is hampered by a lack of experience which she claims to have. Like Square and Thwackum, Mrs. Western and the squire serve as illustrations of the politically narrow-minded. She constantly refers to the sneaking French and the court; the squire sees the current monarch, George II, as bent on sapping money from the country to pay for his grandiose court life, and these are the terms in which they argue. However, like Square and Thwackum, they never really exchange ideas; they only shout at one another.

BOOK VII

Summary

Jones, determining to leave the country immediately, is haunted by dark thoughts: will he ever see Sophia again? Dare he ask her to go with him? Where will he go? What will he do? After thinking about these and other questions, he decides to go to sea and sets out for the port of Bristol.

Meanwhile, Mrs. Western goes to instruct Sophia that matrimony is not an affair of love, but of banking — one deposits one's money where it will reap the most reward. She also tells Sophia that the squire has decided to marry her to Blifil immediately. Sophia absolutely refuses for the simplest of reasons: "I hate him." Mrs. Western, however, remains firm in her brother's resolution and blind to Sophia's tears and entreaties.

During the conversation between Sophia and her aunt, Squire Western is listening at the door, and his temper so overpowers him that he bursts into the room. Mrs. Western is sharply offended, and she and her brother quarrel heatedly about which of them has taught Sophia disobedience. The quarrel ends with Mrs. Western's vowing to leave the estate forthwith. The squire then turns to Sophia and engages her in an argument concerning the virtues, or lack thereof, of his sister. Sophia concludes her defense of her aunt by saying, "So far, sir, from injuring you or your estate, if my aunt had died yesterday, I am convinced she would have left you her whole fortune." These last words penetrate the squire's rage and, indeed, "he started, staggered, and turned pale." After a short silence, Western decides he must attempt to placate his sister. The squire is successful but the result of this reconciliation is that both the squire and his sister turn on Sophia. They decide that the only solution is the prompt marriage of Sophia and Blifil. This decision is given more impetus when Mr. Blifil calls on Sophia that afternoon. Sophia is instructed by her father to receive Blifil well. She does her best, but her behavior is "entirely forced, and indeed such as is generally prescribed to virgins upon the second formal visit from one who is appointed for their husband." Although Blifil appears to be pleased with Sophia's behavior, Squire Western has overheard all and is not pleased. So as Blifil is leaving, the squire says to him, "Allworthy and I can finish all matters between us this afternoon and let us have the wedding tomorrow." Blifil assents, for he has several reasons for desiring Sophia: lust of the flesh, triumph over her spirit, revenge on Tom, and, of course, Mr. Western's estate. He and Western easily convince Allworthy that Sophia is in love with Blifil.

Mrs. Honour, who overhears a conversation between Squire Western and Parson Supple, informs Sophia, whose feelings no one has thought worthy to be counselled, that she is to be wed the next day. Sophia decides to leave her father's house that evening, asking Honour to accompany her. They will go to London to stay with a female relative who has not only invited her, but who also is in favor of women's freedom. They make the appropriate plans, part of which are that, in order to take some of their clothing, Honour will get herself fired. She accomplishes this admirably and swiftly with a few well-placed remarks to Mrs. Western. While Honour packs her (and Sophia's) clothes, Sophia arranges to meet her at a designated place at midnight.

Meanwhile, Tom has some troubles on the road. He hires a guide who, though professing knowledge of the country, has no idea of how to get to Bristol; he succeeds only in getting them lost. Thus Tom takes lodgings for the night and is befriended by a Quaker who tells him of his daughter, a girl who married for love against his explicit wishes. The story sounds so much like that of himself and Sophia that Tom becomes most disconcerted and pushes the gentleman out the door. Shortly thereafter, Tom's guide tells the landlord, and everyone within hearing distance, Tom's history. The landlord refuses to give a bed to such a baseborn fellow as Tom, so Tom is forced to sleep in a chair.

Later that evening, a band of soldiers on the march against rebel forces comes to the inn; the result of this is that Tom volunteers to serve the cause of the king and the Protestant religion for awhile. (The rebellion referred to occurred in 1745; "Bonnie Prince Charles," a descendant of the Stuarts, who held the throne until 1714, attempted to replace George II of the House of Hanover. The revolt failed.) The next morning Tom marches off with the soldiers and, at the end of the day's march, he is invited to dine with the officers. During the meal, one Ensign Northerton begins to harrass Tom about his learning and his gentility. When Tom proposes a toast to Sophia, Northerton declares that he knows the girl and that she "was lain with by half the young fellows at Bath." Tom, incensed, calls Northerton a "most impudent rascal." In response, Northerton throws a bottle of wine which strikes Tom just above the right temple, causing a large gash. Northerton is arrested, and the surgeon prescribes complete rest for Tom.

Tom, who has had a talk with the commanding officer, decides to battle for his honor, and goes to the sergeant to borrow a sword. He then proceeds to the room where Northerton is being guarded by a sentinel. Now Tom presents a strange figure, for his white coat is streaked with blood, his face is pallid from loss of blood, he has a large white bandage around his head, and he carries a sword in one hand and a candle in the other. The guard, filled with terror at this gruesome sight, fires at Tom, but misses, and falls to the floor. Tom then discovers that Northerton has escaped. The guard is blamed for helping the prisoner escape (in actuality, the landlady is to blame), but Tom helps to clear him of the charge.

Commentary

In the introductory chapter to Book VII, Fielding compares the world to the stage. The point of this discussion is basically to emphasize the fact that people are many-faceted and, like actors, play various parts. Therefore, one should not condemn a person simply because of a single bad act. Although Fielding uses the example of Black George stealing Tom's money, the comparison is obviously most relevant to Tom who, in the preceding book, was roundly condemned. Later in the novel, Fielding again uses this metaphor of the stage as a basis for pointing up Tom's rash propensities. In Chapter XIV, after he has been injured by Northerton, Tom decides to seek revenge. The paragraph in which he makes his decision has overtones of Hamlet's soliloquies. Tom, however, is very unlike Hamlet, whose problem is that he can see the arguments on both sides of a question so well that "resolution is sicklied o'er with the pale cast of thought." While Hamlet ruminates for nearly an entire play over the moral questions involved in revenging himself on King Claudius, Tom dispenses with ethics with alarming rapidity:

> . . . and now, having grasped his new-purchased sword in his hand, he was going to issue forth, when the thought of what he was about to undertake laid suddenly hold of him, and he began to reflect that in a few minutes he might possibly deprive a human being of life, or might lose his own. "Very well," said he, "and in what cause do I venture my life? Why, in that of my honour. And who is this human being? A rascal who hath injured and insulted me without provocation. But is not revenge forbidden by Heaven? Yes, but it is enjoined by the world. Well, but shall I obey the world in opposition to the express commands of Heaven? Shall I incur the Divine displeasure rather than be called—ha—coward—scoundrel?—I'll think no more; I am resolved and must fight him.

Here, as mentioned before, is the solution to the majority of Tom's problems: "I'll think no more." If Tom had more of Hamlet's discretion and less brashness, he could avoid most of his difficulties. The parallel to Hamlet is far too obvious to be coincidental; surely Fielding meant for the reader to make the comparison—to Tom's disadvantage. This is particularly ironic in light of the fact that with the stage metaphor in the introduction, Fielding is encouraging the reader to *think* rather than hastily categorize a person or an action. Once again, Fielding is indicating the true norm of sensible actions by juxtaposing two extreme positions, Tom's violence and Hamlet's overcautiousness. This norm is closely akin to the Aristotelian "golden mean."

Finally, it is worth asking oneself why, with the introduction of the Quaker, Fielding virtually retells the story of Tom and Sophia in two pages. It is possible that Fielding is trying to compress most of the events of the novel thus far into a compact unit and, since the story comes from a person the reader hardly knows, one is given an objective examination of Tom and Sophia's courtship. Viewed without bias and in such short space with no distractions, the lovers' problems seem quite simple; in the same way, the greed that prevents their being wed is seen even more starkly in the Quaker's forthright statements. The only correct solution is stated concisely by Tom: send for your daughter and son-in-law and don't be the cause of misery to one you pretend to love. As in many other cases, the word "pretend" confronts the reader. It is interesting that the Quaker never challenges the use of that derogatory word.

BOOK VIII

Summary

The next morning, after the soldiers have departed, the landlady comes up to visit her gentlemanly guest. She speaks flatteringly of Sophia, whose name she has learned from Northerton. Tom is impressed and enthralled with the thought of Sophia. In the course of the conversation, Tom tells the landlady that he is both an orphan and nearly penniless, whereupon she drops all pretenses to civility and unceremoniously departs.

Moments later, the surgeon who dressed Tom's wound arrives and tells Tom that he is seriously ill and the only hope for him is to be bled. Tom refuses, and the doctor retreats to think of other tactics. While speaking to the landlady, the surgeon learns of Tom's near-poverty, so he has a lapse of politeness and concern similar to the landlady's. He rushes into Tom's room and demands payment for services rendered. Tom refuses, and the doctor storms from the room declaiming all such vagabonds.

After a refreshing nap, Tom calls for dinner and for a barber. The barber, Little Benjamin, is well-educated, or so his sprinkling of Latin phrases would indicate, and of a good humor. Tom likes the barber and invites him for a drink after dinner. During their conversation, Tom learns that the barber knows of him. Tom then tells the barber his whole story and, at the end of both the story and the liquor, the barber departs.

The next morning Tom becomes concerned about a new dressing for his wound and is told that the barber is also a skilled physician. So he summons Little Benjamin again and, after his wound is freshly bandaged, Tom requests that Benjamin repay his confidence by narrating his history. Benjamin consents and begins by stating, "You yourself have been the greatest enemy I ever had." Indeed, the barber is none other than Partridge, the schoolmaster charged with being Tom's father. Partridge, however, assures Tom that there is no truth at all to this allegation. He then requests permission to accompany Tom on his travels. Tom, after some discussion of the matter, agrees. Although Tom believes that Partridge offers his services and companionship out of friendship, Partridge actually hopes to persuade Tom to return home and thus regain Allworthy's favor and his old annuity and position as schoolmaster. At any rate, the two depart from the inn the next morning.

After a day of traveling, Tom and Partridge arrive at Gloucester and take quarters in the Bell Inn, where they are warmly received. They have tea with the hostess and Dowling, a lawyer from Somersetshire, and with a knave who thinks himself a lawyer. After Tom leaves the table, the latter tells the others the many stories he has heard about Tom, most of which are grossly exaggerated and the remainder of which are false. Nonetheless, this gives the landlady a dim view of Tom and she begins to be very cool toward him. Tom perceives this change in her attitude and determines to leave at once. He and Partridge travel some distance that night, with Tom sighing and talking of Sophia, and Partridge groaning and complaining of the cold.

After they have traveled quite far, Tom and Partridge see a light near the top of a hill and decide to see if they can stay there for the rest of the night. After much calling and questioning and the promise of half-a-crown, the mistress of the house lets them in. They warm themselves at the fire and comment on the large array of invaluable rarities in the house, but the mistress is visibly upset; she begs them to leave before her master returns. She says that he is not receptive to anyone, keeps entirely to himself, and is known to the neighborhood as the Man of the Hill. Tom is intrigued with the information and asks every question he can think of in order to delay his departure. When he has finally run out of questions and is about to leave, he hears an outcry and several voices. It immediately becomes clear that the master has returned and is being attacked by robbers. So Tom takes up a broadsword and, with a few well-placed blows, fends off the thieves. The Man of the Hill is most grateful and offers Tom anything in his power to give. Tom declines the offer, stating that he has only discharged his duty to a fellow man. After they have conversed for awhile, Tom's curiosity is further aroused by this strange man, so he asks, as repayment for his services, to hear the man's history. The Man of the Hill complies.

In his youth, the Man of the Hill was an intelligent and industrious lad and did exceedingly well in his studies. However, at the end of his fourth year at Oxford, his life style changed abruptly for the worse when he came under the influence of a roguish young man named Sir George Gresham. He was, in fact, easily led astray, for he was "high-mettled, had a violent flow of animal spirits, was a little ambitious and extremely amorous." In short, he began to live a thoroughly debauched life, quickly used up all of his money, and was expelled from Oxford. He then went to London and for two years became deeply involved in gambling. However, his life changed drastically when he rescued a gentleman who had been robbed and beaten. The gentleman happened to be his father and, after a joyous reunion, he returned home with him and resumed his serious studies of the revered, ancient philosophers.

After about four more years, his father died; so unable to live harmoniously with his less studious brother, the Man of the Hill left for Bath. After several most unsavory experiences with ingratitude, treachery, and vileness, the Man of the Hill returned to his cottage where, except for some excursions to the Continent, he has remained. His experiences and his travels have convinced him of one thing only: "Human nature is everywhere the same, everywhere the object of detestation and scorn."

Commentary

In many critical studies of *Tom Jones*, the section of the novel dealing with the Man of the Hill is termed a digression. A number of critics have stated that Book VIII is not directly concerned with the mainstream of the novel. And if one reads *Tom Jones* simply for the story of Tom's loss and eventual regaining of his fortune, in both monetary and amorous terms, then he must surely agree with such pronouncements.

It is true that Book VIII does nothing either to advance or retard Tom's progress, but to conclude that this section is somehow less relevant than other sections of the novel is to commit a critical error against Fielding's warning in the introductory chapter to Book X. Indeed, Fielding's words there are so harsh and so clear that one wonders how anyone could have the courage to use such a term as "digression." Fielding writes: ". . . we warn thee not too hastily to condemn any of the incidents in this our history as impertinent and foreign to our main design, because thou dost not immediately conceive in what manner such incident may conduce to that design. This work may, indeed, be considered as a great creation of our own; and for a little reptile of a critic to presume to find fault with any of its parts, without knowing the manner in which the whole is connected...is a most presumptuous absurdity." Further, to return momentarily to Book I, Fielding's opening remarks establish the fact that he intends to provide a complete sampling of society. This statement of intention, coupled with the tone and thrust of the novel, indicates that Fielding's main concern is with social mores and behavior; that is, the novel is primarily a novel of morals. In this light, the section on the Man of the Hill is extremely pertinent, for it gives us a penetrating glance into a segment of society hitherto unseen in the novel, that of debauched London. Thus, one is able to recognize that London society differs but a matter of degrees from the behavior presented in a number of the characters who have resided on the Allworthy estate. The only difference between the schemes of the brothers Blifil, Master Blifil, Thwackum and Square, and those of the gaming crowd in London is that the latter are more openly corrupt. The same distasteful traits are present in both sets of characters and, if anything, the pretenders to virtue are the greater sinners.

Equally important, Book VIII is a direct comment on Tom's actions and on certain earlier events. Obviously, there is a great contrast between the Man of the Hill and Tom, a difference accurately stated as that of participation versus isolation in society. The question is, which is the more desirable? Tom and the Man of the Hill have similar histories — both were bright, industrious young men and both were prone to rash decisions and had more than their share of what Fielding calls "animal spirits," and both were, as a result of their indiscretions, exiled from their homes. The Man of the Hill has suffered greater consequences, but Fielding has emphasized the similarities of the two men in order to contrast their present attitudes.

The structure of this segment of the novel is important, for the story of the Man of the Hill is enclosed by two scenes: Tom rescuing the man himself and then rescuing Mrs. Waters. Embedded in the Man of the Hill's story are also two rescue stories: he aids his father who has been beaten by robbers, and his last act in society is an attempt to help his friend and erstwhile gambling companion. The irony of the Man on the Hill's philosophy becomes apparent when we note that he is currently engaged in studying the ancient sages. After being saved by Tom's active intervention (for which Tom refuses a reward because he believes he was only fulfilling his duty as a man), the Man of the Hill sits by, even though he — and not Tom — has a gun, while Tom saves Mrs. Waters from Northerton. As we learn from his story, the Man of the Hill has not always been so insensitive to the needs of others, even during his corrupt existence in London. He offered his unsolicited help to his father and was, of course, amply rewarded. As far as mercy and compassion are concerned, and Fielding has repeatedly emphasized the value of these traits, the Man of the Hill is far more deficient now than he was in London. Fielding implicitly states that he has lost rather than gained wisdom, because knowledge gained and not used is worthless. The Man of the Hill is a variety of hypocrite; he roundly condemns society, yet he himself illustrates the same selfish, hypocritical attitudes which he loathes in everyone else and which he does nothing to try to change. To be aware of evil without attempting to eliminate it is surely one of the greatest sins. Thus, Fielding invokes our condemnation of the Man of the Hill in the final scene; in comparison to Tom's gallant, selfless behavior, the Man of the Hill is totally inhuman.

One also must question the validity of the Man of the Hill's pronouncements on society because his sampling has been far too restricted. While living in the corrupt gambling society in London, what could one expect to meet but exactly the kind of people the Man of the Hill describes? Has he not been presented with examples of kind and intelligent people in both his father and in Tom Jones? One can only conclude that the Man of the Hill has made a rash decision on the basis of too little evidence.

Finally, because the Man of the Hill's youth is so similar to that of Tom's, we can make a comparison between his father and Squire Allworthy. The squire totally rejected Tom with far less cause than the Man of the Hill's father. Yet the latter was ready, like the father in the Biblical story of the prodigal son, to receive his son back home. The father amply illustrates the lesson of charity and generosity of soul which Fielding has been working toward. Once again, we find Allworthy, that most generous of men, suffering in comparison to a supposedly lesser man. In effect, Fielding is doing the same as modern-day sociologists and psychologists: laying equal blame on all persons, for none is without guilt.

BOOKS IX-X

Summary

As the Man of the Hill and Tom are returning from a walk to the summit of Mazard Hill, they hear a woman screaming. Tom rushes to her rescue and, moments later, he temporarily incapacitates the lady's attacker. The lady herself is quite disheveled but otherwise unharmed;

her greatest loss is the upper half of her dress. Tom discovers, to his pleasure, that the man who accosted her is none other than Ensign Northerton. He decides to escort the lady and the ensign to the nearest justice of the peace, so he returns to the place where the Man of the Hill has been sitting all this time and gets directions to the local constabulary. While Tom is gone, Northerton escapes, for although Tom bound the ensign's hands, he totally neglected his legs which the ensign uses to escape into the woods.

When Tom discovers he has lost his captive, he decides to take the lady to an inn so that she can regain her composure and borrow some clothes. He bids a hasty farewell to the Man of the Hill and, after a relatively short walk, he and the lady arrive at Upton Inn. The landlady does not like the looks of Tom's barebreasted companion and, in order to maintain the propriety of her establishment, she orders them out. Tom refuses to comply and an argument ensues as the landlord arrives. Upon hearing the landlord hurl a particularly odious epithet at the lady, Tom strikes him and a battle royal begins. Moments later, the fight is joined by the lady in question, Susan (a chambermaid at the inn), and Partridge. The battle might have been longer and bloodier, but it is interrupted by the arrival of a coach and four bearing two young women. Naturally the landlord and his wife immediately disengage themselves to look after their new guests. About this time, a sergeant and a company of soldiers arrive at the inn and demand quarters. The sergeant recognizes Tom's female friend as the wife of Captain Waters and places himself at her disposal. Upon hearing this, the landlady runs to Lady Waters and asks her forgiveness which, after some discussion, is granted. "Matters were thus restored to a perfect calm," comments Fielding.

Tom, who has "a flow of animal spirits which enlivened every conversation where he was present," first turns his attention to oxen and ale and then to Lady Waters, who has been attempting to charm Tom throughout the meal. "To speak out boldly at once," Fielding tells us that Lady Waters is in love with Tom. And since Tom cannot feed upon the presence of his beloved Sophia, he satisfies his appetite with the dish now present. In short, Mrs. Waters' seduction of Tom is quickly accomplished.

While Tom and Mrs. Waters are thus engaged, the company below discusses Mrs. Water's history. The sergeant, who knows her best, claims that she is a good sort and has enough love for Captain Waters — and others. Indeed, there is some doubt as to the validity of the captain's claim upon the lady, for it would seem that they never went through a formal ceremony. We realize now that it was one of Mrs. Waters' assignations with Northerton (during which he decided to rob her) which Tom happened upon.

That evening, after all but Susan retires, an Irish gentleman arrives at Upton Inn in a state of great anxiety and asks whether a certain lady is there. Since the gentleman offers a substantial sum for the answer to his question and, since his description sounds much like Mrs. Waters, Susan directs him to her room. The gentleman breaks the door open and discovers not only Mrs. Waters but also Tom. The gentleman and Tom begin to duel, whereupon the man from the next room arrives and, recognizing the newcomer as a friend, he quickly points out that the woman in Tom's bed is *not* Mrs. Fitzpatrick. Mr. Fitzpatrick sees that he is mistaken and, amidst much embarrassment, begs the lady's pardon. At this point the landlady arrives and begins to scream about the ruined reputation of her house. Mrs. Waters, having regained her composure, says she knows nothing of what has gone on except that she has been awakened out of a sound sleep to find these three men in her room. Tom explains that he came running when he heard Mrs. Waters scream; for that reason only does he now stand before the two ladies in his nightshirt. Mr. Fitzpatrick, thoroughly ashamed of his hasty actions, mutters an apology and leaves the room. Peace is restored once more.

Just as the landlady is about to return to bed, Susan informs her of the arrival of two more guests — a strikingly beautiful, well-dressed young lady and her maid. At the sight of such an obvious person of quality, the landlady makes much ado about getting the lady settled for the remainder of the evening. The pair of ladies is none other than Sophia and Honour.

While taking a meal in the kitchen, Honour learns that Tom is staying at the inn and rushes off to inform Sophia, who, of course, desires to see him immediately. Honour then requests Partridge to call Tom, but Partridge, suffering from the effects of Honour's haughty manner and from a large quantity of liquor consumed earlier in the evening, tells Honour that "one woman is enough at once for a reasonable man." Honour then hurries back and tells Sophia that Tom is in bed with a wench at the moment. This news is extremely vexing to Sophia and, to make things worse, Susan, who is called in for questioning, tells Sophia that Tom has said Sophia is dying for love of him and that he is going to the wars to be rid of her. After vowing eternal contempt for Tom and shedding some tears, Sophia decides to leave the inn at once. But as punishment for Tom, she gives her muff (with her name pinned to it) to Susan to lay on Tom's unused pillow. The next morning, Tom discovers the muff, much to his chagrin. He calls for horses so he can pursue Sophia.

In the meantime, Squire Western, who is also pursuing Sophia, arrives at Upton Inn. When Tom, still carrying Sophia's muff, enters the kitchen, he is greeted with Western's "Halloa! We have got the dog fox, I warrant the bitch is not far off." The cries and rantings of the squire soon rouse everyone in the inn. Among the several guests is a justice of the peace who is prevailed upon to preside over a hearing against Tom, charged with abduction and the stealing of a muff. He is nearly convicted on both counts until he is allowed to testify on his own behalf. Upon the strength of his word, supported by Susan's account of how the muff found its way to Tom's room, he is freed of all charges. As soon as the court is adjourned, the squire leaves in pursuit of Sophia, and so does Tom and Partridge. Mrs. Waters and Mr. Fitzpatrick leave for Bath, "and indeed she did all she could to console him in the absence of his wife."

The last two chapters of the book go backward in time and examine the details surrounding Squire Western's discovery of Sophia's departure and of Sophia's adventures thus far. We discover that, until learning of his amorous adventures at Upton Inn, Sophia has been pursuing Tom. We also learn a relatively important detail which explains why Honour was so ready to condemn Tom:

> . . . Sophia set forward in pursuit of Jones, highly contrary to the remonstrances of Mrs. Honour, who had much more desire to see London than to see Mr. Jones; for indeed, she was not his friend . . . as he had been guilty of some neglect in certain pecuniary civilities, which are by custom due to the waiting-gentlewoman in all love affairs . . . certain it is that she hated him very bitterly on that account, and resolved to take every opportunity of injuring him with her mistress.

Commentary

In several senses, Books IX and X form one unit. First, they both are primarily concerned with the events at Upton Inn. Second, they are a kind of interlude, for though intriguing enough in themselves, they do little to advance the plot. All we learn that is of consequence to the novel is the existence of Mrs. Waters, and that both Sophia and her father are on the same road that Tom is traveling. Obviously, then, the incidents are presented for the sheer interest and vitality that they have in themselves and for what Fielding has termed "the true ridiculous." In other words, we are now into the true picaresque narrative.

Of course, however, Fielding continues his moralizing, enlarging the ideas found in the section concerning the Man of Mazard Hill. As mentioned earlier, Fielding denigrates the sometimes honored position of the recluse as an entirely selfish way of life: the Man of Mazard Hill exists only to fulfill himself; he has renounced society as a lost cause and seeks to concentrate on saving himself. After showing us the hermit in this negative light, Fielding suddenly moves us into the teeming and scheming society which the Man of Mazard Hill has renounced. And at the end of Book X we can clearly see why he chooses to do so. What do we see in these two sections but totally self-centered people? Everyone, from the servants to the gentry, tries to selfishly manipulate others. Both Honour and Partridge, as Fielding illustrates continually, accompany their respective masters only as a means to personal gain: Partridge hopes to guide the errant Tom home and regain Allworthy's favor; Honour looks forward to the wealth and status which life in London can bring her. The landlords and serving people make a fuss over propriety, service, and all such social niceties, but we repeatedly see that they will overlook any behavior and betray anyone if the price is right. The judge, though perhaps not quite so corrupt as the rest, is totally incompetent and only finally does he listen to Tom's evidence. The gentlemen, from the so-called upper class, operate on exactly the same ethical level as the commoners; only their goals are different.

One is forced to conclude that the remainder of society is certainly no less selfish than the man who proclaims his selfishness by resigning from society. Certainly the recluse is more honest; at least he, by his actions, openly demonstrates his selfishness. How then can we condemn the hermit? Certainly one would be at a loss for an answer if he did not realize that comedy often serves to juxtapose the real and the ideal. In each individual case, we judge a character's actions not only against the actions of the other characters but also against an ethical norm carefully established by the author. Fielding is tacitly praising or propounding certain virtues which are the opposite of the vices we see so copiously illustrated. His primary virtues are honesty and generosity of spirit. In accordance with this realization, we can relatively easily place the novel's characters on a descending scale of virtuousness. I stress this point simply because in a picaresque novel, and certainly throughout *Tom Jones*, the unity of the work of fiction is achieved as much through a continuity of moral observations as it is through a continuity of action. In other words, if we want to determine the nature of the cause-effect relationships in this novel, we should not necessarily turn to external actions but to internal motives. As a brief and obvious example, one should be aware that Blifil never gains Sophia's love *not* because he once let her pet bird loose, but *rather* because his desire for her stems from his overwhelming lust for material wealth and from his ardent desires to revenge himself on Tom.

Besides the interest which triggers the kind of analysis given above, Books IX and X surely present one of the most comic passages in English literature, and the comedy exists on at least four levels. First, there is the sheer rapidity with which the events become involved. Characters arrive one after the other until the scene seems on the verge of collapsing into chaos and, after the court scene, they leave just as quickly.

Second, there is the comedy of repetition. Not only do we see innumerable entrances and exits of various characters searching for someone, but there is also comedy in the repetition of the same scene. For example, Mr. Fitzpatrick bursts into Mrs. Water's room, and then Squire Western arrives and he commits the same error. Further, each of the guests (Sophia, Tom, Western, Mrs. Waters, and Mr. Fitzpatrick) bribes the servants and landlady for certain purposes, some of which are diametrically opposed; that is, one character pays to hear a secret which another has just paid to keep quiet. And, of course, there is the repetition of the theme of flight and pursuit. Tom is fleeing and Sophia is pursuing him and, in turn, she is pursued by her father. By the end of the Book X, Tom and Western are both pursuing Sophia, who is fleeing from both of them. For added effect, the reader learns that Mr. Fitzpatrick is pursuing his wife.

This kind of humor, in the hands of Fielding, evolves into hilarious self-revelation: a character, without realizing what he is doing, reveals his real self while actually working very hard to maintain a proper facade. It is due to this comic device that Fielding lets us see really horrible traits — greed, hypocrisy, and incompetence — and still makes us laugh. Our laughter is directed not at the vice as such, but at a character's inability to keep up his mask. Pretensions, when easily seen through, become hilariously funny.

Fielding also uses what can be described as "literary humor" when he invokes the muses, because its success depends on one's ability to recognize the form and Fielding's intentional misuse of it. Traditionally, a poet invokes the muse of poetry to give him the inspiration needed to write about an extraordinarily significant and moving event. To understand what Fielding does, we need only compare the section in Book IX, Chapter V to the opening lines of *Paradise Lost,* in which Milton invokes the heavenly muse to assist him in his difficult task:

> Of Man's first disobedience, and the fruit
> Of that forbidden tree whose mortal taste
> Brought death into the World, and all our woe,
> With loss of Eden, till one greater Man
> Restore us, and regain the blissful Seat,
> Sing, Heav'nly Muse . . . .

Particularly noteworthy is Milton's undertaking: to "justify the ways of God to men." Fielding's purpose, on the other hand, is to "say what were the weapons now used to captivate the heart of Mr. Jones," the first of which is "two pointed ogles." Fielding burlesques both literary tradition and his characters by using style which is wholly unsuited to the seduction scene. Into that very style, Fielding inserts very ordinary and deflating words, like "ogle" and "the coarse bubbling of some bottled ale." To use Fielding's own metaphor, all of these factors add up to a most delightfully concocted literary repast.

Before moving on, one would do well to consider the mock trial. The state of English common law was one of Fielding's most serious concerns. As mentioned earlier, Fielding, as both lawyer and magistrate, directed a great deal of his energies toward promoting an equitable judicial system. At this relatively early stage in his life, he was still willing to try to change certain social ills by holding them up for derisive laughter. As he grew older, he became more venomous in his writings, as in many passages in *Amelia.* Interestingly enough, it seems that Fielding moved from his basically active, Tom Jones-like stance to a more bitingly sarcastic position, similar to that of the Man on the Hill. One must not, of course, take the comparison too far, since Fielding was literally killed by his numerous projects to correct social injustices. He was never a misanthropic hermit.

BOOKS XI-XII

Summary

After Sophia leaves Upton Inn, she travels but a few miles before she is pursued and overtaken by two ladies on horseback. The ladies are Sophia's cousin, Mrs. Fitzpatrick, and her maid. Sophia and Harriet Fitzpatrick are delighted to meet, for long ago they lived together with their Aunt Western. They soon take accommodations in an inn and begin to acquaint each other with their reasons for being on the road.

Briefly, Mrs. Fitzpatrick's story is that while on a holiday in Bath, she became infatuated with and married Mr. Fitzpatrick, only to discover that the rogue had married her for her money. (In fact, Fitzpatrick courted both Harriet *and* her aunt, but chose Harriet "on account of her ready money.") Her only excuse for having made this dreadful match is that "it requires a most penetrating eye to discern a fool through the disguises of gaiety and good breeding." He abused her verbally, kept a mistress, and finally lost all of their money in gambling debts. When Harriet refused to sell a small estate, her husband became irate, accused her of infidelity, and locked her in her bedchamber. Luckily, she managed to escape.

The two young ladies are interrupted in their exchange of tales of woe by the sounds of an altercation downstairs. Honour comes raging into the room, declaring that she has bodily attacked the landlord because he said Sophia was Jenny Cameron, whore of the pretender to the throne, Bonnie Prince Charles. The truth is that the landlord was suspicious of a lady of quality who was traveling so secretly. He made innumerable innuendoes to Sophia, but she thought he had somehow learned of her real identity and was referring to Squire Western rather than to Prince Charles. Sophia's true identity is loudly established by Honour, who refuses to be called the waiting-woman to a whore.

After tranquility returns once again to the inn, the landlord announces that an Irish peer is below. The peer is none other than the gentleman who assisted Harriet in her escape from her husband. He so hates tyrants, whether husband or father, that he offers both Sophia and Harriet the use of his coach and six for their continued flight. His offer is graciously accepted. Thus, they arrive in London in style and procure lodgings. Harriet takes rooms at the expense of the Irish peer, who, Sophia has reason to believe, is on rather intimate terms with Harriet. Sophia moves into the home of Lady Bellaston, a good and sympathetic friend of the Western family.

After Squire Western leaves Upton Inn, he begins to bemoan his fate—not so much for losing Sophia, but for having to waste such a fine hunting day. However, luck is on his side; he travels hardly any distance before he hears the familiar sound of a pack of dogs. Unable to restrain himself, he joins the chase and spends the rest of the day with his new-found friends. The next morning, he is dissuaded from further pursuit of Sophia principally because he has no idea which way she went.

Meanwhile, Tom has also departed from the inn and, after much bitter complaining about his most recent separation from Sophia, he finally declares, "Since it is absolutely impossible for me to pursue any farther the steps of my angel — I will pursue those of glory. Come on, my brave lad, now for the army." Partridge, being basically in love with his own life, is quite reluctant to go to war. He and Tom are debating this issue when they happen upon a beggar, to whom Tom promptly gives a schilling. The beggar offers to sell Tom a book which he found. When Tom inspects it, the first thing he notices is the signature of Sophia Western; the second is a 100-pound note which falls from the book. Tom is overjoyed but also apprehensive, for he fears Sophia will need the money before he can find her.

Soon after they leave the beggar, Tom and Partridge hear the sound of a drum, and Partridge immediately concludes that they are being overtaken by rebel forces. Tom, however, believes the drums are emanating from a village celebration. Indeed, the noise comes from a puppet show in a nearby town, where Tom and Partridge take lodgings.

Later that evening, while Tom is discussing the virtues of the stage with the landlord of the inn and the owner of the puppet show, he hears a quarrel in the adjacent room. The cause of the disagreement is that the landlady has discovered her maid and the jester from the puppet show "in a situation not very proper to be described." The landlady proceeds to curse both the maid for her whorish behavior and the owner of the show for the bad example he sets with his puppet plays. The landlady's accusations effectively silence the puppet master's discourse on the virtues his shows impart to the general public, so he has no recourse but to find his Merry-Andrew and punish him. At length, however, all parties are reconciled.

Tom retires to bed and the rest of the company to the kitchen for conversation. Partridge begins by declaring that he believes Tom to be slightly mad. Everyone except the landlady agrees and feels that perhaps Tom should be bound and taken home. But as no one is willing to attempt to bind such an apparently spirited young man, the conversation moves on to the subject of the rebellion, concluding with the observation that everyone's first consideration is his own purse.

The next morning, Tom is awakened out of a sound sleep by the noise of a fight outside his window. He discovers "the master of the puppet-show belabouring the back and ribs of his poor Merry-Andrew without either mercy or moderation." Tom, of course, interposes, but he has no sooner quieted the master than the jester begins to harangue, reminding his master that by dissuading him from robbing a beautiful lady yesterday, he has saved him from a hanging. Tom soon learns that the lady in question is Sophia and he is eager to be off once again on her trail.

Tom and Partridge have just set out when they are overtaken by a rainstorm. In the ale house where they take shelter, Tom discovers a boy who has recently been Sophia's guide. Tom persuades him to escort them to the inn where he left Sophia; but, upon arriving there, he discovers that Sophia has just departed. He does find a friend, though; Mr. Dowling, the lawyer, has recently taken lodgings there. While Tom is waiting for his horses to be refreshed, he shares a bottle of wine with Dowling. The lawyer persuades Tom to relate what has happened, and Tom complies, ending his monologue with, "I feel my innocence, my friend; and I would not part with that feeling for the world." Then Tom and Partridge and their guide depart for Coventry.

The night is very dark, the rain is coming down in torrents, and the trio soon lose their way. With every step, Partridge asserts that they have been bewitched by an old hag at the inn to whom Tom failed to give a donation. Finally, they see lights ahead and as they draw nearer they hear strange music. Partridge is sure this is a meeting of spirits, witches, and hobgoblins. Actually it is a celebration of a band of gypsies who receive Tom and his companions with the utmost hospitality. While Tom is discussing various things with the gypsy king, Partridge is seduced by one of the gypsy women. Unfortunately, her husband catches them in a most embarrassing position, so Partridge is brought before the king. Tom offers to pay the wounded husband, but the king, who learns that the husband has been spying on his wife all evening, declares he should have had enough love to interrupt the seduction much earlier. The king punishes both the husband and the wife. Tom declares this to be the best system of justice he has ever witnessed.

After the rain ceases, a gypsy guide leads Tom and his party to Coventry. From there, Tom travels, always close on the heels of Sophia but never catching her, to Daventry, Straford, Dunstable, and St. Albans. At St. Albans, they stop at an inn and, while dining, Tom tells Partridge that they have but little money left. Partridge replies that the 100-pound note will buy any number of meals. Tom becomes incensed at the thought of spending Sophia's money and attacks Partridge's ethics, declaring that he will never be dishonest enough to spend the money— even if it belonged to someone other than Sophia.

This matter being settled, Tom and Partridge leave the inn. Not long after they have been on the road again, they are overtaken by a would-be robber. Tom gives him all the money he has, except for Sophia's bank note which he refuses to surrender. Then Tom manages to wrestle the gun from the rather incompetent robber. After he has been subdued, the highwayman tells Tom that the pistol is not even loaded and that this is his first robbery, attempted only because his family is starving. Tom advises the man to find more honest means of helping his family and gives him two guineas.

Commentary

Books XI and XII form a symmetrical unit; each contains the same amount of time and each takes our hero and heroine from Upton Inn to London. Both books contain picaresque adventures and use a gamut of comic devices, from mistaken identity to bawdy humor to the now familiar subject of Partridge's unnecessary fears.

Book XI introduces a new character, Mrs. Fitzpatrick. This incident serves to give the reader a deeper look into the character of Mrs. Western, the squire's sister. Equally important, the history of Mrs. Fitzpatrick gives the reader a picture of the kind of matrimonial disharmony from which Sophia is running. One sympathizes with Sophia's actions since her proposed marriage to Blifil, which was founded on greed, would probably have been as unfortunate as Harriet's marriage. Further, the portrayal of the intrigue, cunning, and gossip at Bath foreshadows the London society to which we are about to be introduced.

There are two sections of Book XII which deserve close attention. The first of these is the discussion of low material and "idle trumpery" on the stage. The main point, as stated by the stage master of the puppet show, is that his puppet shows serve to improve the morals of society. He vows never to introduce "low stuff" on his stage. Fielding obviously does not agree with the puppet show's moral worth because his own "low stuff" immediately follows (the affair of the chambermaid and the Merry-Andrew). Not only is this scene hilariously funny, but it deftly contradicts the point that the stage master is making; his puppet show, though void of all low stuff does nothing to improve the morals of even his own clown. Fielding here is ridiculing the pious prudes of his era, those who lambasted the stage as a major cause of the decline in morals.

Fielding's point here is twofold: not only are people's ethics developed quite independently of the stage, but perhaps the word "moral" needs to be redefined. Fielding implies throughout the novel that actions in and of themselves are neither moral nor immoral; rather, one must judge the motives behind the actions. For example, one need only examine Fielding's attitude toward the robber, whom Tom meets in Book XII, and Mr. Fitzpatrick. Also, it is safe to say that the only times in the novel when Fielding condemns a sexual relationship is when one person is being used as an object rather than as a human being, as is the case in Tom's future relationship with Lady Bellaston and in Fitzpatrick's marriage to Harriet.

Finally, the episode involving the gypsies is instructive of Fielding's moral viewpoint. In the person of the gypsy king, we see what approximates an ideal ruler. The society over which he presides is far superior to that in which Tom lives; no one is ever hungry or without clothing or shelter; the king's justice rivals that of Solomon. The reader can easily see Fielding's point, since he is already acquainted with Black George Seagrim and his family, and particularly since he just witnessed a man forced by poverty to become a robber. Through this method, Fielding's novel is a critique of his society. Further, the incident with the gypsies is reminiscent of Jonathan Swift's *Gulliver's Travels*, which was published twenty-three years before *Tom Jones*. The main characters, Lemuel Gulliver, visits four strange lands and his experiences are a direct comment on English society. Gulliver, like Tom and the gypsy king, discusses the methods of ruling and the state of the societies which he visits. The major difference between Swift's writing and Fielding's, however, is that the tone of *Gulliver's Travels* is frequently bitter and savage, and it vascillates between humor and horror because it is filled with several images of man as a grotesque oddity in the world of nature. Fielding's touch, as always, is extremely delicate and although harsh criticism is implied, it is not prolonged and is frequently mitigated by the humorous antics of Partridge.

In the scene with the gypsies, Fielding enumerates the three qualities which make a superior leader: moderation, wisdom, and goodness. But these are the qualities which Fielding has promoted for everyone throughout the novel, so the moral lesson quickly moves from the particular discussion of rulers to the proper behavior for all mankind. Fielding's satire in *Tom Jones*, with its burlesque and subtle ironies, never becomes venomous or vengefully directed at a particular personality. He attempts not to alienate his readers by abusing them, but to make them laugh at their own follies.

BOOK XIII

Summary

Tom arrives in London in the evening but is unable to find the lodgings of the Irish gentleman who befriended Sophia and Mrs. Fitzpatrick. The next day his luck is somewhat better, for he finds not only his lordship's dwellings but also those of Mrs. Fitzpatrick. Since Tom is a handsome fellow and admirably well mannered, Mrs. Fitzpatrick receives him. But thinking that he is an emissary from Western in behalf of Blifil, she denies all knowledge of Sophia's whereabouts. Nonetheless, she agrees to see him again. After Tom leaves, Mrs. Fitzpatrick's maid says that the gentleman must be the Mr. Jones of whom Honour has spoken. After she has heard all that Honour relates about Tom, Mrs. Fitzpatrick thinks it best to try to save Sophia from such a rake. Further, she also thinks that if she can persuade Sophia to forget Tom and return home, she herself will gain not a little favor from both the squire and his sister. Thus, she decides to acquaint Lady Bellaston, with whom Sophia is staying, with Tom's character. Lady Bellaston. however. has already heard about Tom from her own servant, Mrs. Etoff, who had heard of him from Honour. Lady Bellaston is most curious about this lad whom everyone describes with so many superlatives; she begins to think of him as "a kind of miracle in nature." Not surprisingly, she tells Mrs. Fitzpatrick that it would be easier to prevent Tom from courting Sophia if she could have a look at him. Mrs. Fitzpatrick is able to grant this request since Tom is soon calling upon her.

When Tom does call that evening, he is received most graciously. And while he is there, Lady Bellaston sweeps in, followed by the Irish peer. Tom is only a spectator to the polite conversation which follows and, after leaving his address with Mrs. Fitzpatrick, he departs. When he calls again the next day, however, Mrs. Fitzpatrick refuses to see him. The reason, which Tom does not know, is that the Irish peer has forbidden her Tom's company. After attempting to see her several times that same day, Tom returns to his lodgings.

Tom has taken rooms at the home of a clergyman's widow, Mrs. Miller, of whom Squire Allworthy always spoke highly. So hither Tom returns after his unsuccessful entreaties. As he is contemplating his bad fortune, he hears an uproar downstairs and a female voice calling on him to prevent murder. Tom, as usual, quickly responds to such cries of distress and runs downstairs. There, a "gentleman of wit and pleasure" is pinned to the wall by his footman. Tom rescues the victim, Mr.

Nightingale, who no sooner recovers his voice than he fires the footman. He then thanks Tom and insists that they share some wine. While drinking, he explains that he struck his footman because the fellow mentioned the name of a young lady "in such a manner that incensed me beyond all patience." Tom agrees that this is sufficient reason. Soon the lady of the house and her two daughters join them, and they spend a delightful evening together. Mrs. Miller is so charmed by Tom that she invites both men to breakfast with her the next morning.

While they are at breakfast, a porter delivers a package for Tom. The parcel contains a mask, a masquerade ticket, and a card which reads, "To Mr. Jones: The queen of the fairies sends you this; Use her favours not amiss." Tom thinks he is receiving the favors of Mrs. Fitzpatrick, and Mr. Nightingale, thoroughly delighted with Tom's stroke of luck, offers to accompany him to the masquerade.

When they arrive, Tom, who hopes to meet Sophia there, speaks to every lady he sees in order to try and recognize Sophia's voice. While he is thus engaged with one lady, another whispers to him that if he does not stop flirting, Miss Western will learn of it. Tom's heart leaps and he, sure that this is Harriet, implores her to tell him where Sophia is. Although Tom gets no reply, he does get a very strong hint that the disguised lady is interested in filling in for Sophia. So Tom, not exactly invited or excluded, follows the lady to an apartment where he discovers that the masked lady is not Harriet, but Lady Bellaston. Their meeting, which lasts most of the night, consists "of very common and ordinary occurrences" and, at the end of it, another engagement is arranged for the following evening.

After Tom has slept off his night-weariness, he arises and gives Partridge 50 pounds, a gift from Lady Bellaston, telling him to have it changed. That afternoon, while at dinner, Mrs. Miller tells Tom and Mr. Nightingale of her relatives whom she has visited that day. They are destitute, starving and sick. Tom gives her the 50 pounds, telling her to use as much of it as necessary to mitigate their circumstances. She will accept, however, only a part of Tom's generous gift.

That evening, Tom returns to Lady Bellaston's apartment and the same "ordinary occurrence" transpires. Although Tom sees much of Lady Bellaston in the ensuing days, he learns nothing of Sophia's whereabouts. In fact, Lady Bellaston begins to refuse to mention Sophia's name. Tom then asks Partridge to inquire of the lady's servants. In the course of his relationship with the lady, Tom, through her violent affection for him, becomes one of the most affluent people in London.

One evening just before he is to meet Lady Bellaston at her home, Mrs. Miller asks him downstairs to meet the relative whom he aided. The relative is none other than the would-be robber, but Tom does not mention this, and says only that the man is an acquaintance. Tom learns that the man's family is much better now, having beds, food, and improved health. Tom is jubilant at the news, and his emotions soar as he rides to Lady Bellaston's home.

When he arrives, the lady has not yet returned and, while waiting for her, he meets Sophia, who was sent to a play but returned early. Tom and Sophia meet in the drawing room and both are dumbfounded. Recovering his faculties, Tom returns Sophia's book and money and asks her pardon. Sophia severely rebukes Tom for having bandied her name about the countryside. Tom assures her that he has not done this at all and concludes that the culprit must be Partridge. "This point being cleared up, they soon found themselves so well pleased with each other that Jones quite forgot he had begun the conversation with conjuring her to give up all thoughts of him." Then Lady Bellaston walks into the room and is as startled to see Tom and Sophia together as they were to discover each other. She recovers her composure very quickly, however, and pretends not to know Tom at all. Tom explains his presence by the necessity for returning the book and money and, as a reward for so doing, asks for the pleasure of a second visit. Lady Bellaston does not refuse. On his way out, Tom meets Honour and gives her his address.

Commentary

With Book XIII, the reader moves into the third major section of the novel—that of the city. As noted earlier, Fielding constantly works in terms of juxtaposing one thing against another and, besides the many characters that can be fruitfully compared, one should also compare the effects of the various settings on the major characters. Tom and Sophia have lived in the country and traveled the road and, although they have met many pitfalls, Tom has been only slightly marred and Sophia is totally unscathed. But once they arrive in London, the situation alters radically. Tom becomes a kept man; he is selling his body to Lady Bellaston, whom he does not love. Sophia, too, suffers her first fall from grace, and Fielding tells the reader at the end of this section of the novel:

As for Sophia, her mind was not perfectly easy under this first practice of deceit; upon which, when she retired to her chamber, she reflected with the highest uneasiness and conscious shame. Nor could the peculiar hardship of her situation, and the necessity of her case, at all reconcile her mind to her conduct; for the frame of her mind was too delicate to bear the thought of having been guilty of a falsehood, however qualified by circumstances. Nor did this thought once suffer her to close her eyes during the whole succeeding night.

Tom's ethical lapse is, of course, the greater by far, and the qualifying circumstances that he is doing it in an attempt to gain knowledge of Sophia does nothing to mitigate his sin. In effect, it makes it worse because he is using Lady Bellaston as a means rather than as a person, a respected entity, complete in herself. Fielding does, however, show us that Tom has not basically changed, for one sees this in his ready generosity.

Fielding does not long leave the reader in the dark about the nature of the evil in the city. Tom succumbs to the blatant deceit and pretentiousness that fills the air of London. The first hint of the evils of city life occurs when Fielding describes Mr. Nightingale, a member of society who is totally useless because he does nothing constructive. Even when confronted with an obvious case of great need, his compassion compels him to offer but one guinea, and even this is a token gesture since he does not actually offer the coin itself. Nevertheless, Mr. Nightingale is a member of the upper class and is a "gentleman of wit and pleasure"; Fielding, in one of his most sarcastic turns of phrase, translates this to mean men of wisdom and vertu (power), those who spend their hours conquering the science of gambling, learning the subtleties of bribery, and writing speeches for publication in magazines in order to make these accomplishments seem admirable.

The second and most significant indication of the nature of city life is the section concerning the masquerade. This scene seems to epitomize the corruption of London which Fielding wishes the reader to see; nearly everyone he portrays hides behind a mask. Thoughts which are not "polite" are left unspoken; life among the wealthy is as ritualized and formal as the masquerade. One must put on the proper disguise, and Tom's attendance at the masquerade is extremely significant. As soon as he conforms with the practice of masquerading, the mask proves contagious and, even though he never had "less inclination to an amour than at present," he begins to answer Lady Bellaston in increasingly warm and suggestive tones. He falls into the clutches of

Lady Bellaston, is trapped into a kind of prostitution, and covers his basic nature with embellished finery which the city has to offer. Yet one tends not to condemn Tom's actions because, after all, the novel is a comedy; but most comedy does have serious implications to which the reader must attend if he is to feel the full significance of the work.

The reader should have noted that in the chapters set in the city, Fielding's writing becomes the most "heavy-handed" and the moral framework of the novel becomes more obvious. One need read only a few of the descriptive passages in this section to discern the great distaste from which they stem. The following quotation from Book XIV, Chapter I is an example of Fielding's bluntness:

> The highest life is much the dullest, and affords very little humour or entertainment. . . . except among the few who are engaged in the pursuit of ambition, and the fewer still who have a relish for pleasure, all is vanity and servile imitation. Dressing and cards, eating and drinking, bowing and curtsying, make up the business of their lives.... In my humble opinion, the true characteristic of the present beau monde is rather folly than vice, and the only epithet which it deserves is that of frivolous.

This is indeed a sweeping condemnation.

BOOK XIV

Summary

That same evening Tom receives two letters from Lady Bellaston, both of which display her extreme displeasure at Tom's meeting Sophia; the second, however, makes plain her desire to see Tom again. Before Tom has time to respond to the lady's invitation, she comes to his room and rages at him. She has hardly begun when Partridge announces the arrival of Honour with a letter from Sophia. Mrs. Honour spends not a few minutes lambasting the character of Lady Bellaston, leaving the lady, if possible, even more enraged. At length, Tom pacifies her with protestations of innocence and assures her that his meeting with Sophia was entirely accidental. Before Lady Bellaston leaves, she decides Tom should now meet her at her house. This greatly pleases both parties: Tom is glad to be able to see Sophia at any cost, and Lady Bellaston is pleased to have Tom's visits imputed to Sophia's charms; thus "she herself would be the person considered as imposed upon."

Sophia's letter to Tom implores him not to visit the house lest they be found out. So, the next morning, Tom sends a letter to Lady Bellaston saying he is ill and cannot keep the appointment. Shortly before noon, Mrs. Miller comes to visit Tom. She informs him that if he intends to have female visitors until two in the morning, she will have to ask him to leave, despite her respect for both him and his foster father, Squire Allworthy. Tom tells her that if his guests are to be controlled, he will find other lodgings, and sends Partridge to do so.

Mr. Nightingale comes to Tom's room to tell him that he too is leaving; his father has arranged for him to marry a lady of fortune whom he is to meet shortly. Tom rebukes Nightingale for courting Nancy, Mrs. Miller's daughter, only to disappoint her, but Nightingale assures Tom that he does love Nancy but that he must follow his father's wishes or lose his inheritance. Tom accepts this explanation, and the two agree to take lodgings together. The next day, however, Tom learns from a most distraught Mrs. Miller that Nancy is pregnant, has attempted suicide, and that Nightingale has disappeared. Tom, after promising to aid Nancy, finds Nightingale, who is in the depths of despair. He wants to marry Nancy, but because of his honor and his father, he cannot. Jones then undertakes to persuade the elder Nightingale to permit the marriage.

Unfortunately, when Tom locates the elder Nightingale, the gentleman has just finished negotiating with the father of the future bride, and "fortune could not have culled out a more improper person for Mr. Jones to attack with any probability of success." Nevertheless, Tom, with a few well-placed compliments, wins the gentleman's favor temporarily and then tells him that his son is already married to Nancy. Hardly has Tom spoken these words than Mr. Nightingale's brother comes into the coffeehouse. The brother has come to dissuade Mr. Nightingale from pursuing the match he seeks for his son, because, in the opinion of the brother, the lady is "very tall, very thin, very ugly, very affected, very silly, and very ill-natured." In spite of both Tom's and the brother's wise counsels, Mr. Nightingale will not be reconciled to his son. When Tom leaves, the brother Nightingale accompanies him to Mrs. Miller's so that he might speak with his nephew. When he does, he learns the whole truth and immediately attempts to persuade his nephew *not* to marry Nancy. Nightingale steadfastly refuses to follow this advice, but does agree to go home with his uncle for the night.

Commentary

Book XIV basically serves as relief for the reader from Tom's entangled affairs; the reader now becomes concerned with the fortunes of

Nightingale and Mrs. Miller. But like the Quaker's story in Book VII, Chapter X, it reminds us of the basic problem that Tom must soon battle, because Nightingale's story is similar to Tom's: an avaricious father impedes the course of true love. Also like the Quaker's story, the roles are reversed and it is the lady who is socially inferior and it is the gentleman's father who interferes. In terms of structure, then, Fielding has set the novel so that during Tom's adventures on the road, when we are concerned with people other than those who represent a direct stumblingblock to Tom's marriage, the hero's story is framed by incidents which recapitulate the central issue. In this way, Fielding keeps the major plot mechanism before the reader in spite of all of the distracting incidents. As stated earlier, this device of repetition allows the reader to see the central issue objectively, without the confusion of such appealing characters as Squire Western.

This section of the novel also illustrates Tom's consistency and his sincere concern for the emotional and financial welfare of others. He is consistent in that he still advocates love over monetary considerations. He is concerned primarily with the consequences of Nightingale's actions on poor Nancy. Though Partridge can jest about Nancy's delicate state, Tom has a true sensitivity to others and, in Nancy, he rightly sees that if Nightingale deserts her, it could have a calamitous effect. His position is vindicated when Nancy attempts suicide after reading her lover's farewell letter. Tom senses sincere emotion, but a lack of fortitude in Nightingale. So he boldly, as always, wades in to calm the troubled waters.

This section, then, serves to reaffirm our faith in Tom's good natural instincts. When the welfare of another is at stake, he instinctively does the right thing. The timing here is important, for this comment on Tom is made just before nearly everyone's opinion of him declines rapidly.

BOOKS XV-XVI

Summary

While Tom is attending to Nightingale's affairs, Lady Bellaston attends to his. She arranges for Lord Fellamar, who has fallen deeply in love with Sophia and desires to marry her, to rape Sophia. Lady Bellaston does this believing that Sophia's hand will go where her chastity goes; thus she will be rid of her rival for Tom's affection. The plot is carefully laid, and Lord Fellamar and Sophia are left entirely alone in the apartment.

Fortunately for Sophia, the lord is interrupted from his ardent work by the unexpected entrance of Squire Western. He is, not surprisingly, intoxicated. As soon as he sees Sophia, he begins to chide her for her disobedience and insists that she return to Sommersetshire and dutifully marry Blifil. Lady Bellaston comes in at this point and, seeing that one means to the desired end is as good as another, begins to support the squire's demands on Sophia. The squire then demands that Sophia come with him to his lodgings; on the way out, he insults Honour for having helped Sophia escape. (The squire, incidentally, learned of Sophia's whereabouts from Mrs. Fitzpatrick, who desired a reconciliation with the squire and his sister.)

While Tom is sitting with the Miller family, after the departure of Nightingale with his uncle, Honour arrives to acquaint Tom with all of the foregoing events. While Honour is there, Lady Bellaston's arrival is announced. Tom, hopelessly disconcerted, hides Honour behind a curtain. The lady then comes in and begins to make soft, warm advances to him; Tom, of course, can say nothing since Honour is but a few feet away. He is rescued from this embarrassing position by the drunken entry of Nightingale. After Tom takes care of Nightingale, he returns to his room only to find that Lady Bellaston, in attempting to hide, has discovered Honour. However, since the lady could hardly suspect anything between Tom and this servant, the air is soon cleared, and Lady Bellaston retreats, though not without a certain amount of haughtiness.

The next morning, Tom has the pleasure of serving as a stand-in father for Nancy Miller in her marriage to Nightingale. Afterward, Nightingale, remembering Tom's evening visitor, tells him the history of Lady Bellaston, consisting mostly of her amorous dealings with numerous young men before Tom. Nightingale assures Tom that the word "honor" has no meaning when the subject is Lady Bellaston, so Tom begins "to look on all the favours he had received rather as wages than benefits . . . and he determined to quit her." Nightingale then assures Tom that the speediest way of ridding himself of her is to propose marriage, so Tom does so by a letter. The scheme works and Tom is overjoyed, even though his freedom also means penury.

That same day, Mrs. Miller also receives a letter—it is from Allworthy and informs her of his and Blifil's impending arrival in London and of their desire for lodgings. To make room, Jones and Nightingale and Nancy move into the rooms the men had taken before the wedding.

Tom is further surprised on this day by a sudden proposal from Mrs. Arabella Hunt, a wealthy widow who lives next door to the Millers and who has seen much of Tom and greatly liked what she has seen. Even though Tom now feels the pinch of his dwindling wallet—and Mrs. Hunt's fortune is most enticing—he refuses her kind offer, stating that his heart is in the hands of another. While Tom is feeling virtuous about his decision, Partridge arrives with the news that Black George is among the servants whom Western has brought to town and that he has just spoken with him. Tom decides to have George deliver a letter to Sophia.

After recapturing his daughter, Squire Western again implores her to marry Blifil and, when she refuses more adamantly than ever, the squire imprisons her in her apartment. On the second day, an emissary from Lord Fellamar speaks to Squire Western and asks permission for the lord to court Sophia. The squire refuses in rather rough language, so the emissary informs him that the lord will require satisfaction in the form of a duel in Hyde Park that very morning; with this demand, the emissary gives the squire "a manual remonstrance." The squire then dances about the room bellowing, levying insults, and revoking them at the same time. At this point, the emissary indignantly states, "I see, sir, you are below my notice, and I shall inform his lordship you are below his," and leaves. Sophia, who has heard all this but has seen none of it, begins to scream. The squire rushes to her room and, when each discovers that the other is unharmed, they resume their argument over Blifil. The scene ends with Sophia collapsing into a chair amidst a storm of tears while her father looks determinedly down at her.

When Black George serves Sophia her dinner that evening, he also serves up the letter from Tom, for he has carefully placed it into the breast cavity of the fowl. The letter contains Tom's ardent protestations of love. Sophia, however, cannot respond because she has neither paper nor pen.

Sophia is soon rescued from her imprisonment by the timely arrival of her aunt, who immediately demands full charge of the affairs of Sophia. The squire, thinking again of his sister's estate, acquiesces. Mrs. Western frees Sophia and takes her to accommodations more suited for persons of quality. No sooner has Sophia acquired her freedom than she writes a letter to Tom.

Meanwhile, Blifil and Allworthy arrive in London and pay a visit to Squire Western. To be sure, Allworthy has serious misgivings about the match when he learns that Sophia has run away to avoid marrying Blifil. But Mr. Blifil's cunning tongue and well-pretended sincerity persuade

Allworthy to visit the Westerns again. Western, of course, wants Blifil to see Sophia immediately, but Mrs. Western insists that Blifil follow decorum and arrange such affairs in the proper manner.

During this time, Lady Bellaston has not been idle. She tells Lord Fellamar that she will aid his suit for Sophia and then informs Mrs. Western of the lord's intentions; the squire's sister is highly pleased. Lady Bellaston, according to Fielding, has that strictly feminine desire not to see a former lover belong to anyone else, so she requests that Fellamar dispense with "that vagabond Jones" by having him pressed into military service. To provide a margin of safety, she also gives Mrs. Western Tom's recent letter of proposal. Mrs. Western agrees that once this is shown to Sophia, her love for Tom will diminish considerably.

Now Mrs. Fitzpatrick, whose scheme for reconciliation with the Westerns has been a total failure, decides to revenge herself on the squire and his sister. Thus, she asks Tom to pay her a visit. Though Tom does not agree to her proposed plot, an unfortunate end comes to his visit; as he is leaving the house, Mr. Fitzpatrick is approaching it. Being of an insanely jealous nature, Fitzpatrick immediately draws his sword and demands satisfaction from this man who has cuckolded him. The result of the battle is that Tom delivers what is pronounced as a mortal blow, is taken before a magistrate, and from there to jail. Not long after Tom arrives at this odious institution, Partridge delivers him a note from Sophia in which she discloses knowledge of Tom's affair with, and proposal to, Lady Bellaston. The letter ends, "All I desire is, that your name may never more be mentioned to me."

Commentary

Perhaps the only possible comment on the action in Books XV and XVI is that the plot thickens so quickly that it takes one's breath away. It is obvious that Fielding is used to writing for the stage, for he is a genius at piling dramatic event upon dramatic event. He continually leaves one wondering what he could possibly do next and how he can possibly unravel all of the thoroughly entangled plot threads.

In the introductory chapter to Book XV, Fielding provides some foreshadowing of the events to come. He mentions the old belief that "virtue is the certain road to happiness" and, although he discounts it as totally invalid, it is exactly what happens in the history of Tom Jones, who indeed finds true happiness after embracing virtue and wisdom. But Tom's path to happiness is a most circuitous one and, in Book XVI, one of his stops along the way is the jail. But Fielding has already prepared the reader for this eventuality: ". . . nay, sometimes perhaps we shall be obliged to wait upon the said happiness to a jail, since many by the above virtue have brought themselves thither." Fielding thus mentions the depth of Tom's disgrace and the final happiness to which he will rise.

Once more, one should note the fine balance between the comic and the serious that Fielding manages to maintain. As Tom's luck rapidly declines, the comic scenes continue to provide relief and tantalize the reader's emotions. In Book XVI, for example, one finds two scenes inserted solely for sheer delight: the scene with Western and Lord Fellamar's messenger, and the portrait of Partridge at the theater. Although the former does have a vague relation to the plot, the latter has none at all and is meant only to be thoroughly enjoyed. There is also interspersed throughout these chapters the continuing battle between Squire Western and his sister, and it is no less funny now than it was at the beginning of the novel.

BOOK XVII

Summary

The next morning at breakfast, Mr. Blifil begins to tell Allworthy of the recent incarceration of the villainous Tom. Upon hearing this, Mrs. Miller cannot keep silent. She praises Tom for his gentleness, warmth, and kindness and is about to tell the whole story of Tom's sojourn at her home when Western comes rushing in. He is in a fit of pique about the suit of Lord Fellamar. He urges an immediate and forced wedding ceremony. Allworthy will not allow this at all and, in fact, suggests that Blifil drop his courtship of Sophia altogether. Western is displeased, and he and Blifil convince Allworthy to let time take its course, hoping that Sophia will change her mind.

By now, Mrs. Western has become as intent on Sophia's marrying Fellamar as the squire is on Sophia's marrying Blifil. Mrs. Western insists that her niece receive Lord Fellamar. Sophia, however, by means of some well-placed flattery, obtains the agreement of her aunt not to leave her alone with the lord.

In the meantime, Tom's friends visit him in his confinement and cheer him immensely. They tell him that Fitzpatrick, though critically injured, is not yet dead. Mrs. Miller also agrees to deliver a letter to

Sophia. And she does more; she tells Sophia all that Tom has done to help her family. Unfortunately, however, the maid overhears Mrs. Miller's story and tells Mrs. Western of it. This enrages the lady who, after voluminous and furious words to Sophia, declares that she will have no more to do with the matter and will deliver Sophia back to her father the very next day.

Tom's fortunes now move up and down rapidly. He learns from Mrs. Miller of his rejection at the hands of Mrs. Western. Then he receives a most unexpected visit from Mrs. Waters, the lady whom he saved from Ensign Northerton, and with whom he spent an enjoyable night at Upton Inn. Mrs. Waters has met Fitzpatrick and has become his mistress. She now tells Tom that there is no chance that the man will die; furthermore, Fitzpatrick firmly owns up to being the cause of the unfortunate battle. Tom is, to say the least, highly pleased.

Commentary

As the plot gains momentum, events occur with almost confusing rapidity, but by the time the reader finishes Book XVII, he realizes that there is enough matter in suspension to allow for a happy ending when it all settles. Tom is cleared of murder, he is a little redeemed in Sophia's eyes, and he is even rising in Allworthy's estimation.

More important, we are witnessing a change in Tom's character. Since he received the news from Sophia that she learned of his proposal to Lady Bellaston, Tom has begun to realize the fact of cause and effect and that he must accept the consequences, however painful, of *all* of his actions. He is sincerely penitent for his rash and thoughtless acts and realizes that not only have they lost him Sophia, but they have inflicted emotional pain on others. He is beginning to learn the lesson that Allworthy, when he was near death, said Tom must learn: the value of prudence and wisdom. Tom now knows that he must gauge beforehand what the results of a particular act will be. In other words, though the plot has not yet reached its climax, the moral framework has; once Tom has gained prudence and wisdom, he is surely destined for happiness. Then he will be worthy of Sophia. Tom has moved from innocence to a fallen state and, by virtue of his many experiences, has gained a higher state. One should, at this point, reread the introductory chapter to Book XIV, in which Fielding very explicitly remarks on the absolute necessity of experience to the learning process: "A true knowledge of the world is gained only by conversation. . . ." Although he is speaking in terms of art, surely he means these remarks to be applied to the story of life in this novel. After all, working from Fielding's implied literary theory here, what is art but a reflection of the human experience? If this is the case, then, one's observations on art are equally applicable to life.

With the development of Mrs. Miller's character, we are presented with another truly good person who serves to point up Allworthy's imperfect perceptions. Though she has but little education, she is the one who quickly discerns which side of Tom's character is the truer. She knows which acts to overlook and which to emphasize. Allworthy, on the other hand, has allowed himself to be persuaded to ignore the good and magnify the bad parts of Tom's personality. Nor is Mrs. Miller fooled by Blifil's oily tongue; her perception is based on feeling and experience rather than on theoretical justice. Fielding's irony works at its most subtle level when Allworthy gives Western a patient, condescending smile because of his stupidity when he himself, in refusing to hear Mrs. Miller's remarks against Blifil, has been equally narrow and silly.

BOOK XVIII

Summary

As soon as Mrs. Waters leaves and Tom is meditating on his somewhat precarious state, Partridge, in a shockingly disheveled state, rushes into Tom's cell. With an expression of utter horror on his face, Partridge asks Tom if the lady who just left was the Mrs. Waters at Upton Inn. Tom says that she is and that it is hardly a secret that he has been to bed with her. Partridge cries, "Why, then, the Lord have mercy upon your soul, and forgive you, but as sure as I stand here alive, you have been a-bed with your own mother." Tom is dumbfounded, but Partridge assures him that Mrs. Waters is none other than the former Jenny Jones. As soon as Tom recovers his voice, he dispatches Partridge to find the lady and fetch her back to him. Although Partridge has no luck in this quest, Tom does receive a letter from Mrs. Waters; she tells him she will take the first possible opportunity to see him.

On the next day, Allworthy goes to the elder Nightingale, for he promised Mrs. Miller he would attempt to reconcile father and son. His visit meets with much success on that score. Further, while he is there, he sees Black George Seagrim who, so Mr. Nightingale says, has managed to save a very tidy sum. Allworthy is quite surprised and, when Nightingale shows him the bank notes, Allworthy recognizes them as those which he gave to Tom. On returning to his lodgings, Allworthy finds that Dowling, the lawyer, is with Blifil; indeed, the two spend much time together. Allworthy asks Dowling what can be done in a case of theft of bank notes. Dowling says that since he has business there anyway, he will put the question before counsel. Then Mrs. Miller comes in with the news of Tom's innocence, and Allworthy admits that he is glad to hear this and that perhaps he may "be brought to think better than lately I have of this young man."

Later that day, Allworthy receives a most sober, honest letter from Mr. Square, who has recently taken ill and is now on his deathbed. In the letter, Square, to repent for his sins, frees Tom of much of the guilt which has been laid against him, particularly of the ingratitude he was accused of on the occasion of Allworthy's grave illness. Ironically, Allworthy receives by the same post a most indignant letter from Thwackum, still in the best of health, who abuses Tom's character. He enjoins Allworthy to forget Tom, then requests the post of a vicar who, it is rumored, is not far from the grave.

Mrs. Miller enters and tells Allworthy the truth about the villainy done Tom by Lord Fellamar in attempting to press him into service. Also, Allworthy learns that Dowling has been seen in the company of the very soldiers who framed Tom. Allworthy confronts Blifil with a direct question about Dowling's dealings with the soldiers. Blifil, though momentarily caught off his guard, recovers quickly and invents the tale that Dowling was trying to soften the witnesses' statements against Tom. Blifil's fast answer here is easily explained, says Fielding, for the devil "generally stands by those who are thoroughly his servants, and helps them off in all extremities. Allworthy then decides to visit Tom in jail. As they are about to leave, Partridge arrives and, learning of the plan, tells Mrs. Miller of Tom's latest misfortune, that of incest, and says she must stop Allworthy from visiting the prison because the sinning mother and son are at this moment bemoaning their crime. Mrs. Waters informs Allworthy that Tom's servant advises that it would be best not to visit Tom just now.

Allworthy wishes to speak with Partridge in order to hear the whole story of Tom's travels. The result is that Partridge assures Allworthy that he is not Tom's father and then tells Allworthy of Tom's committing incest. Hardly has Allworthy recovered from the shock when Mrs. Waters comes in. She then tells Allworthy the truth about Tom's parentage: Tom is the son of none other than the squire's own sister, Bridget, and was fathered by a Mr. Summer, a clergyman's son who lived at Allworthy's home until he died, a few months before Tom was born. Allworthy, convinced of the truth of Jenny's story, responds with,

"Good heavens! Well! the Lord disposeth all things." Jenny Jones then says that Bridget always intended to tell Allworthy the truth, but finally thought it unnecessary since Allworthy seemed so fond of Tom. But, Jenny continues, she never dreamed that Tom would be prosecuted unjustly by a lawyer hired by Allworthy. At this, Allworthy is astonished, especially when he further learns that Dowling has attempted to bribe Jenny to testify against Tom.

Squire Western blunders in, raging against "that bastard Tom"; he has discovered Tom's most recent letter to Sophia. Allworthy says he will speak to Sophia about the impending marriage.

As Western leaves, Dowling comes in and is startled to see Mrs. Waters. When Allworthy questions Dowling, he finds that it was Blifil who sent him upon the mission to undo Tom and that he also bribed the officers who witnessed the fight between Jones and Fitzpatrick to testify that Tom was the cause of the fight. Allworthy also learns that while he was ill, his sister instructed Dowling to deliver Allworthy a letter in which she explained the facts of Tom's parentage; Blifil received the letter and never showed it to Allworthy. Allworthy is at last convinced that Blifil is "the worst of villains."

As he promised, Allworthy pays a visit to Sophia. But contrary to Western's expectations, he tells Sophia that he is extremely glad that she has escaped from what would have been a miserable marriage to a villain. Allworthy then begins to advance the cause of his nephew Tom, but Sophia, without stating any reasons, resolutely refuses to see Tom.

When Western comes in, he blusters about the room upbraiding Sophia. Then Allworthy tells him all he has recently learned. As soon as Western discovers that Tom is to be the heir to the Allworthy estate, he is as eager for Sophia to marry Tom as he had been for her to marry Blifil. Allworthy counsels moderation, but he does finally agree to bring Tom to visit them the next day. When Allworthy returns to his lodgings, Tom is already there, and a very tender scene of reunion occurs. Tom vows that he has seen the errors of his actions and that he has received only the punishment which he deserved. Allworthy replies, "You now see, Tom, to what dangers imprudence alone may subject virtue . . . Prudence is indeed the duty which we owe to ourselves." He further states that imprudence can be corrected but such villainy as Blifil's is irretrievable.

Squire Western, who cannot wait to see Tom, calls at the house. When Allworthy goes down to receive him, Mrs. Miller comes to inform

Tom that Nightingale has explained to Sophia that the condemning letter to Lady Bellaston was not sincere, but was only an invention meant to repel rather than to attract the lady. In spite of the explanation, Sophia remains resolved to forget Tom.

After the squire leaves, Blifil sends word to ask Allworthy if he may see him. Allworthy is enraged and is about to disavow all allegiance to him but Tom intervenes and bids him be merciful. Allworthy is astonished at the depth of Tom's goodness. Allworthy then informs Tom of Black George's theft. Tom is surprised, but he attributes it not to greed but to George's desire to see his family provided for. Allworthy is again astounded at Tom's goodness, but reminds Tom that robbery alone is sometimes excusable, but when it is accompanied by ingratitude, it is unforgivable.

The discussion is put to an end because it is time to visit the Westerns. In brief, the result of this visit is that Sophia, after some hesitation, agrees to marry Tom. The next morning, Tom and Sophia are married, and happiness prevails, for the Nightingales have also been reconciled. The day and evening are spent with much mirth, highlighted by occasional songs from Squire Western "which bore some relationship to matrimony and the loss of a maidenhead."

After thus concluding his narrative of Tom Jones, the author summarizes what later happened to the rest of his characters:

Although Allworthy would never again consent to see Blifil, he did, at Tom's behest, bestow a tidy annuity on Blifil, and Tom secretly increased it. Blifil moved to a northern town and turned Methodist in hopes of marrying a wealthy Methodist widow. Also, he is attempting to make the necessary monetary and political arrangements to buy a seat in parliament.

Square soon died, but Thwackum continues to live and to attempt to regain Allworthy's confidence by constantly flattering him to his face and abusing him behind his back. Allworthy, however, has taken a Parson Abraham Adams into his house in Thwackum's place, and Sophia has become so fond of him that she declares he will tutor her children, a boy and a girl.

Mrs. Fitzpatrick, with the help of her Irish peer and Lord Fellamar, has obtained a separation from her husband and is living in London and "is so good an economist that she spends three times the income of her fortune without running in debt."

The elder Nightingale has purchased an estate near Tom's for his son, who, with his wife and Mrs. Miller, lives in great harmony with the Joneses.

When Black George learned that his crime had been discovered, he left for parts unknown. Tom gave the money to George's family; Molly received the largest portion.

Tom gave Partridge a fifty pound annuity and Partridge established a school. "There is now a treaty of marriage on foot between him and Miss Molly Seagrim, which, through the mediation of Sophia, is likely to take effect."

Squire Western gave his estate to Tom and Sophia and moved to better hunting country. He visits his family quite frequently, and they adore him and delight in pleasing him. He dotes on his two grandchildren, and "the old gentleman declares he was never happy in his life till now."

As for Tom, his conversation with Allworthy and his marriage to "the lovely and virtuous Sophia" have quite overcome all of his tendencies to vice; he has thus "acquired a discretion and prudence very uncommon in one of his lively parts."

Commentary

The narrative has come full circle. Everyone has returned to the country and once again leads a blissful life: paradise has been regained. Now, all evil has been removed; there is no Blifil, Square, Thwackum, nor even a Black George to disturb this virtuous existence. The evil remains in the city with Mrs. Fitzpatrick, the Irish peer, and Lady Bellaston, all of whom, Fielding hints, continue in their same worthless pursuits. Thus the restored Eden is fulfilled even down to the total separation of virtue and vice. Further, the picaresque hero has fulfilled his quest; he has gained Sophia and has regained his true birthright as master of the land.

The conclusion of *Tom Jones*, with its vision of a cleansed and perfected society, not only fills the demands of the comic genre but also represents the mainstream of eighteenth-century philosophy. The eighteenth century is referred to quite frequently as the Age of Reason because the prevailing beliefs of the era were centered on an implicit faith that man is a perfectly rational being by nature, and that evil is but a lapse of his natural rationality. The reader need but skim through the book to see how frequently Fielding refers to the power of reason and how often he points out unreasonable actions or beliefs; reason plays a major role in the moral framework of *Tom Jones*. Indeed, irony, which is by far Fielding's most frequent comic device, is based on the supposed rationality of the reader, because in order for it to be effective, one must be able to discern, through a basically logical process, the subtle differences between two sets of behavior. One must be able to work in an almost syllogistic fashion from the implied premise to the implied conclusion of a particular statement or action. Further, the essential moral lesson that Tom learns is a lesson in logic: one must be able to see the pattern of cause and effect; that is, one must learn to establish a consequential relationship between his own actions and ensuing events. More important, one must be able to reason out the future consequences of a proposed activity in order to determine the morality of that action. The conclusion of the novel is overwhelmingly optimistic in that it asserts the possibility of attaining this kind of bliss. (Remember that Fielding, in several introductory chapters, as well as throughout the novel proper, firmly asserts that he is but writing from experience and in imitation of nature itself.) Similarly, eighteenth-century philosophy firmly asserts that man can perfect his society if he but follows his rational *instincts*. Alexander Pope, in his *Essay on Man*, best summarizes this belief:

> Whether with Reason, or with Instinct blest,
> Know, all enjoy that pow'r which suits them best;
> To bliss alike by that direction tend,
> And find the means proportion'd to their end.
> . . . .
> Take Nature's path, and mad Opinion's leave
> All states can reach [Happiness], and all heads conceive;
> Obvious her goods, in no extreme they dwell,
> There needs but thinking right and meaning well.

In other words, reason is one of man's basic instincts and, to be happy, he needs only to follow it. As soon as Tom begins to think, his fortunes begin to change for the better simply because he is in harmony with his environment. By the end of the novel, Tom resides in complete harmony because he is following his rational instincts, those which lead to virtue and happiness.

CHARACTER ANALYSES

TOM JONES

Tom Jones is basically a "growing up" novel; that is, we witness the maturation of the hero of the novel. However, the maturation itself occurs rather rapidly, to say the least, and it occurs in the opening chapters of the concluding book. For the first seventeen books of the novel, Tom remains a healthy and sensitive adolescent.

Tom's actions consistently indicate the impulsive nature of youth and stem from a *carpe diem* philosophy. His desire for unrestrained expression of his feelings, immediate gratification of his needs, and immediate corrective action for the injustice he sees — all these reflect the spontaneity and idealism typically associated with youth. Tom's actions are a series of unpremeditated, impulsive responses based on emotion rather than on analysis. Thus, while he is madly in love with Sophia, he can spontaneously go to bed with Molly Seagrim, Mrs. Waters, or Lady Bellaston. There is no contradiction in these actions since he is concerned with the eternally present *now* rather than with an unrealized and unplanned future. His plan of action never extends beyond a day or two and, even when he decides that the solution to his problem is to go to sea or join the army, he can just as easily change that plan in the next moment.

Tom's character is, however, infused with a sincere concern for the welfare of others. One must be careful not to say "welfare of mankind" here, for Tom does not think in abstractions; he responds only to immediate and specific examples. Thus, while one never hears Tom philosophizing about the state of man, he does see him impulsively giving aid to Black George, the Man of the Hill, Mrs. Waters, Mrs. Miller's relatives, Nancy Nightingale, and all at some cost to his own welfare, both physical and financial. He does respond negatively to the Man of the Hill's absolute condemnation of man and positively to the gypsy king's philosophy of paternal benevolence, but, by and large, this is only because he has specific instances of behavior to work from. He knows the Man of the Hill is wrong because he has seen Allworthy at his best; he can appreciate the gypsy's justice because it is overwhelmingly fair to poor Partridge, who, ironically enough, was condemned by Allworthy for the very same "crime."

It is, of course, Tom's unmitigated imprudence which forms the basis of conflict in the novel. The primary conflict is internal, and the external conflict between Tom and Blifil or Western is only the superficial manifestation of the conflict within Tom himself. He continually brings about his own troubles simply because his preoccupation with the present does not allow him to see the relationship between past, present, and future. By acting on the spur of the moment, Tom never pauses to ask how one action will affect other actions and other people. Even though he desires Allworthy's approval, he impulsively commits deeds which bring Allworthy's disapprobation; though he desires Sophia's affections, he sometimes acts as if his love for her were only one of several such "loves." It does not take a cunning Blifil to make fornication, inconstancy, and prostitution look bad, and these are the "sins" of which Tom can rightfully be accused.

Tom, however, does finally realize that he has been acting as if deeds are committed in a temporal and ethical vacuum. When he discovers that he has had a sexual relationship with a lady who is supposedly his mother, his world of innocent action comes crashing down about his ears; he realizes the profundity of his guilt and the consequences that his impulsive, unquestioning actions can have: "But why do I blame Fortune? I am myself the cause of all my misery. All the dreadful mischiefs which have befallen me are the consequences only of my folly and vice." Tom's use of the word "consequences" here is the first instance of a recognition of a causal relationship between events. By acting on this recognition, Tom can move to improve his situation; by the end of the novel, he has become a thoroughly prudent, thoroughly wise squire. The final picture of Tom is that of a man who has harmonized all aspects of his life. He has recognized the continuity of time, the eternal presence of past, present, and future and has assimilated the societal values of prudence and decorum, so ardently preached by Allworthy.

Tom's immense appeal as a character is due primarily to two factors. First, he is full of enthusiasm, optimism, and energy. He fully enjoys living, even, one feels, when he is in the depths of despair about his seemingly futile love for Sophia. Second, it is easy to identify with Tom because he is of that class of heroes who, as Northrop Frye has remarked, belong to a basically realistic vein of literature and are on a par with the reader because they suffer from the same limitations and follies. Tom is an "everyman."

MR. BLIFIL

Blifil is in every way Tom's foil. He has none of the impetuosity of youth and none of Tom's idealism or generosity. He is a portrait of the thoroughly evil and thoroughly selfish man. Even when we see Blifil, at the tender age of thirteen, release the bird which Tom gave Sophia, it is not merely a childishly taunting incident. It is a cleverly planned scheme to put Tom in a bad light; in other words, Blifil is "thirteen going on forty." As Tom is concerned with the present, Blifil is obsessed with the future; his every activity, from extreme obeisance to his tutors and uncle to his scheme to hide the truth of Tom's paternity, is part of his plan to inherit as large a share of the Allworthy estate as he possibly can. He is so thoroughly aware of the causal nature of events that he manipulates them to his own best advantage. In fact, he is so busy manipulating that he can never enjoy living; all of his joy is pinned on one moment in the future, and that moment, justly enough, never arrives.

Unlike Tom, Blifil does not learn from experience and does not gain a proper perspective on time. At the end of the novel, he is engaged in exactly the same kind of activity that we have seen throughout: he is scheming to acquire a fortune. The only difference is that the estate belongs to a Methodist widow rather than to Allworthy. While Tom is full of healthy "animal spirits," Blifil is "wholly of the devil's party."

SQUIRE ALLWORTHY

As his name suggests, Squire Allworthy is supposedly a master of all the virtues — wisdom, goodness, justice, generosity, mercy, and godliness. He sincerely attempts to live up to his name. We cannot doubt his generosity, for he is quite free with both his home and his money. However, because of his abstract concepts of justice and morality, we can doubt his wisdom, or at least his perception.

Allworthy is what one might call a conservative interpreter of the Mosaic laws. He has bound himself and others, in his position as magistrate, to strict observance of this code and thus his justice is one of rules and regulations rather than a more humanistic assessment of the circumstances in each situation. Therefore, when the evidence seems to point to one conclusion, Allworthy does not question the source of his evidence — as indeed he should have in the case of Partridge's wife and of

Blifil's continuing testimonies against Tom. Allworthy's errors would not be so glaring if Fielding had not introduced two distinct contrasts to the kind of justice Allworthy deals out. The first is that of the Man of the Hill's father who forgives his son and welcomes him home though he has committed deeds far worse than Tom's. The second is the gypsy king who seems to assess injustice as any failure of love. Thus, when Partridge is found in a compromising position with another man's wife, the gypsy king condemns the husband for not loving his wife enough to keep her from seeking gratification elsewhere and for not stopping the affair earlier. Allworthy is guilty of a lack of perception simply because he never considers possible motivations, but only the actual fact of guilt. Since he never looks behind the surface of "facts," he is easily duped by the appearance of virtue and sincerity. It is his concern with appearances which leads him to condemn Tom. It is his concern with appearances which allows the schemes and disguised greed of Captain Blifil, Thwackum, Square and Mr. Blifil to pass by him unnoticed until they have caused a great deal of damage to others. The kindest remark we can make about Allworthy is that he does sincerely attempt to establish a strongly ethical code for himself and that he is unafraid to admit his errors.

SQUIRE WESTERN

Squire Western is obviously a man much given to the enjoyment of life, but only on his own terms. He is robust, rowdy, lusty, vulgar, and eminently delightful simply because he manages to infuse his every waking moment with a profound *joie de vivre*. One feels that Western absolutely and thoroughly enjoys everything he does—from hunting, drinking, eating, listening to Sophia play the harpsichord, and even arguing violently with his sister. He, like Tom, has enough of youthful spontaneity to leave the serious business of pursuing his daughter in order to join a fox hunt.

Because of his immense energies, however, Western is also both a domineering and stubborn figure. Once he has established a course of action, nothing can turn him from it. After deciding that marriage to Blifil is in Sophia's best interest, no one can convince Western otherwise; even Allworthy with his quiet eloquence cannot persuade Western that Sophia should have a choice in the matter. Western does not counter any opposition with logical arguments, he simply and energetically reasserts his opinion. When he finds himself in a logically untenable position, he only shouts more loudly.

Since Western, like Tom, is a firm believer in the efficacy of immediate and direct action, he is one of the more physically oriented characters in a novel teeming with mental schemers. When confronted with a distasteful situation, Western's first response is always a physical one: he bodily assaults Tom, he flings Sophia's muff into the fire, he locks Sophia in her room. It is this impulsive behavior which gives him the flavor of youth and makes him seem more akin to Tom than any other character in the novel.

MRS. WESTERN

Mrs. Western, like her brother, has boundless energies and she has directed most of them toward gaining knowledge of the world. She is well-read in literature, both contemporary and classical, and she keeps up with the flood of political pamphlets pouring from the presses in London. She has had some connections with life at court and she is decidedly a royalist. Further, she makes the most of all such connections, however minor, and continually compares her brother's conduct of his estate to the conduct at the court—always, of course, to indicate what a boorish, uncultured bumpkin the squire is. She is also a perpetual and incurable adviser, even when her advice is unsolicited and unwanted.

However, one must admit, as Fielding readily does, that Mrs. Western's knowledge is entirely theoretical since she has had no practical experience in either politics or romance. While her feminine decorum has stopped her from actively entering the realm of political action, her masculine virtues have prohibited romance: "either she had no inclinations, or they had never been solicited; which last is indeed very probable; for her masculine person, which was near six foot high, added to her manner and learning, possibly prevented the other sex from regarding her, notwithstanding her petticoats, in the light of a woman."

She and her brother, like Square and Thwackum, make ideal fighting companions for they hold opinions diametrically opposed and are not at all reticent to voice them loudly. While the squire is basically an earthy country squire, fond of the pleasures of the body, Mrs. Western is concerned with artifice, the social graces and the appearance of good breeding. She works under the illusion that she herself is infused with the air of the court and insists that that air be maintained wherever she is. She is "a perfect mistress of manners, customs, ceremonies, and fashions," but she is *not* a mistress of personalities and subtle nuances of emotions. She sees every act as a kind of ruse and insists on viewing everyone else in terms of her own affectations.

SOPHIA WESTERN

Sophia is, of course, the soul of beauty, womanhood, and sincerity. She is a loving and obedient daughter and becomes a loving and obedient wife. As Fielding remarks, she has "the plain simple workings of honest nature." Within these "workings," however, she has the ability to love deeply and to assert her independence of body and spirit. But, she also has grace and charm enough even to win unwittingly the admiration and affections of a London nobleman. She is, in other words, not unschooled in the feminine arts.

As we learn during her journey to London, Sophia has inherited some of her father's energies. She has enough spirit to deny both her father's and her aunt's demands, to undertake a rather dangerous journey to London, and to show Tom what his activities with Mrs. Waters lost him by leaving her muff on his unused pillow. One must admit that she has more of understanding and mercy than most lovers; she forgives Tom innumerable instances of inconstancy, indeed, almost as if she did not expect fidelity. Like the virtuous woman that she is, she can forgive Tom anything but his bandying her name about the country and thus staining her reputation. But since it is Partridge and not Tom who is guilty of this, all is set for her final acceptance of Tom.

One must finally admit, however, that he cannot delve too deeply into Sophia's character for she is the least fully realized of the novel's major characters. Only briefly and early in the novel, do we see Sophia's concern for the welfare of others: she likes Tom greatly because she has heard of his efforts to aid Black George's family, and she herself gives Molly some clothing from time to time and offers her a job in her house, and is eager to comply with Tom's request that she ask her father to give Black George a job. Of her intellectual achievements, we have only Fielding's statement that "her mind was every way equal to her person; nay, the latter borrowed some charms from the former."

It has been argued that Fielding left the outlines of Sophia's character purposefully vague so that the reader could imagine her more attractive. By not limiting her with a thorough description, Fielding allows the reader to mold her according to his own ideals. Perhaps this line of argument has merit, but nevertheless it is perfectly obvious that Fielding meant for her to be an ideal person. In fact, his portrait of her is said to be a tribute to his late wife who had died in 1744, for Fielding says of Sophia, "...most of all she resembled one whose image never can depart from my breast, and whom, if thou dost remember, thou hast then, my friend, an adequate idea of Sophia." She is the one character in the novel whose traits are never burlesqued and whose actions are never condemned.

MR. PARTRIDGE

As Tom's traveling companion and supposed father, the bumbling Mr. Partridge is a thoroughly comic figure. And, as the inept but pedantic scholar, he is also a stock comic character, having an analogue in comic satire as early as Aristophanes' play *The Clouds*. Partridge partakes of the stock figure of the rather cowardly and unintentionally clownish servant and, of course, he is the counterpart of Don Quixote's companion, Sancho Panza.

These stock traits more or less define Partridge's character, which is never intended to be subtle. He is the ardently earnest man who takes himself far too seriously and thus can only be seen comically. Partridge, however, is basically appealing because of his winsome, naive simplicity and because of his sincere concern for Tom. In the same moment, he can be both pompous and declarative and his ill-informed opinions on any number of subjects from Latin to the theatre and can also exhibit petty, superstitious fears of being overtaken by witches and hobgoblins. In the next instant he can throw himself wholeheartedly into battle for Tom, as he does at Upton Inn. Typically, his battle is with the chambermaid, and he loses.

THWACKUM AND SQUARE

The two scholars in the Allworthy household have the same fundamental traits and are as easily confused with each other as are Hamlet's undefined friends, Rosencrantz and Guildenstern. They both live in the Allworthy home simply for the advantage it brings them, as their obvious and ingratiating preference for Blifil, the young heir to the fortune, so easily illustrates. Although Thwackum speaks continually of piety and Square of virtue, neither is as concerned with such abstractions as they are with the material reality of the pound sterling. Although Thwackum is a devout, orthodox Anglican and Square is a thoroughgoing deist, it makes no difference in how they conduct their lives. Neither ever listens to the logic that is presented by the other nor to the logic which they themselves spout; they simply respond on cue with memorized phrases. Fielding states it quite precisely:

Upon the whole, it is not religion or virtue, but the want of them, which is here exposed. Had not Thwackum too much neglected virtue and Square, religion, in the composition of their several systems, and had not both utterly disregarded all natural goodness of heart, they had never been represented as the objects of derision in this history.

(Book III, Chapter IV)

Square does, however, redeem himself through his totally unexpected confession to Allworthy of his and Thwackum's misrepresentation of Tom's actions. Thwackum, however, remains as hypocritical, dogmatic, and ungrateful as ever.

GENERAL COMMENTARY

STRUCTURE AND THEME

There are basically three types of artistic structure in *Tom Jones* which are ingeniously combined into one large framework. The form of the novel is so well integrated with the thematic content that one finds it extremely difficult to discuss one without discussing the other, so the following commentary on the novel's structure will necessarily include a discussion of the moral implications of these structures.

The first structural level is that of mere plot incident, the movement from one event to the next. One must remember that Fielding is caught between two opposing literary types in constructing *Tom Jones*. First, in calling his novel an epic, Fielding more or less binds himself to the literary tradition established by Homer in *The Iliad*. This tradition, as expounded by Aristotle, dictates a "unity of action"; that is, the entire plot of the work must be a unified whole connected by discernible causal relationships. The reader should be able to pinpoint the cause of each event. In the first section of *Tom Jones*, roughly through Book VII, this description is apt. One can easily see that the misinterpretation and misrepresentation of Tom's actions cause his disfavor with Allworthy. One event leads logically to the next, and the result of all the incidents is Tom's expulsion from the Allworthy estate. However, in the next section of the novel, we find that the focus of the action shifts, and that Fielding is following a different tradition, that of Cervantes' picaresque novel, *Don Quixote*. This latter literary form is related not to the classical epic but to the medieval romance. Essentially, the romance is but a series of heroic adventures which are connected only by the fact that they happen to the same person. Obviously, this is an apt description of Tom's journey to London—he moves from the band of soldiers to Mazard Hill to Upton Inn to the gypsies to London with one incident having little or no causal relationship to the next.

Interestingly enough, the novel's final section combines both of these structures. Fielding introduces several characters (for whom he provides a full background in the epic style) who are at best only tangentially related to Tom's story—Harriet Fitzpatrick, the Millers, and Mr. Nightingale. Also, some of the final twists of the plot seem to be added because Fielding delighted in illustrating his dexterity in resolving such complexities. A good example is Lady Hunt's proposal. Other scenes, like that of Partridge at the theater, are included for the sheer delightfulness of their humor. However, the final section not only has the direct causal relationship between the affair with Lady Bellaston and Tom's further alienation from Sophia, but Fielding also provides some of the plot's missing links. With our knowledge of Mrs. Waters' identity, we learn the importance of the hitherto disconnected affair at Upton Inn, as well as the significance of the trial of Jenny Jones which opens the novel.

The importance of this kind of literary experimentation cannot be overestimated. Since Fielding's work occurred at the formative stages in the history of the novel, his freedom with structure, his eclectic nature, and his disdain for critical rigidity virtually assured that the novel would never be a sharply defined genre.

On another structural level, Fielding experimented with the traditional epic structure by placing it within a larger comic structure. One should remember that Fielding had examples of both the epic and the mock-epic forms in Milton's *Paradise Lost* and Pope's *The Rape of the Lock*. Perhaps Fielding realized that the obvious next step was to put the epic into a form which would be as relevant to his society as *The Iliad* was to Homer's.

Traditionally, the epic has the following characteristics: (1) a hero who is of great significance; (2) the action contains deeds requiring an extreme amount of valor and skill; (3) the setting is of vast scope; (4) supernatural agents become involved in the action; (5) the style is consistently elevated; (6) the narrator-poet remains objective in recounting the story; (7) the action begins *in medias res;* and (8) the narrative contains lists or catalogues of ships, warriors, and weapons, and is often interrupted by background stories of various characters. It is easy to see how Fielding altered these characteristics to suit his particular purposes. The hero, as mentioned in the introduction, is of great significance in that he is, as a foundling, from the ranks of the masses, and his actions are significant in that they are, at least potentially, experiences of everyone. Such other characteristics as invocations of the muses and catalogues have been discussed earlier when they occurred in the novel. One epic trait which Fielding uses and which is structurally important is the biographical sketches of characters only vaguely related to the central plot—notably the Man of the Hill and Mrs. Fitzpatrick. As in the epic, such seeming digressions serve two purposes: they retard the movement of the narrative in order to create a higher pitch of suspension and they offer an indirect comment on the major action of the story.

It is important to note that Fielding's adaptation of the epic structure results in a literary form designed and directed specifically to the broad spectrum of the English public. The literary form which Fielding created is just as culturally instructive as *The Iliad* was to the Greeks. However, what is being celebrated is not the triumphs of a national military hero, but the triumph of a cultural hero, *the common man*, represented by Tom Jones (note the extraordinary commonness of his name alone), who is a foundling. One might term Fielding's work the democratization of the epic.

Another element which profoundly affects the novel's form is the comic structure, which dictates that none of the pretentious epic devices are to be taken seriously. To assure a continuous and consistently comic tone, Fielding adheres to the principle that he states in the introduction to Book V; that is, he alternately presents sober and comic passages. Yet there are subtle relationships between these passages; frequently, a comic passage will contain material which is an ironic comment on a serious statement made earlier. The effect is to make the comic tone much more pervasive and, since much of the humor depends on irony, to make the comic structure extremely intricate.

The third structural level is that of the novel's allegorical elements. And when dealing with allegory, one must be extremely careful to observe the plausible limits of the allegory's utility in describing a work of art. By definition, an allegory is a set of one-to-one relationships between persons and things in the narrative and between ideas and persons outside the narrative. For example, in political satires, one often sees characters who obviously represent various figures on the current political scene: Mr. Powderdupe might represent the president, Mr. Gunshaker might be the secretary of defense, and a murky, muddy pond in which the action takes place might represent the political realm as the author sees it. However, when the literary work moves away from such an obvious level and becomes more intricate in structure, one must not insist that the allegorical overtones are the final and definitive description of the work. Rather, they are only one of several substructures of the novel and are not an absolute statement, but simply a relatively important factor which the critical reader must consider.

As noted in the introduction, one can see *Tom Jones* as an allegory of the redemption of man; it is, at least from one point of view, an indication of Fielding's interpretation of the Christian virtues. The movement in the novel is obviously one of Tom Jones' going from a state of innocence at the beginning of the novel through many experiences into the painful world of guilt. The climax of the redemptive movement occurs while Tom is in jail and learns that he is supposedly guilty of incest. The lesson here is that Tom has not passed through the temptations of the world unscathed; he has sinned and, had not *chance* intervened, could very well have committed this most heinous sin. The problem, as Fielding states repeatedly is *not* that Tom is evil; on the contrary, his motives are superlatively generous and his emotions sincere. The problem is Tom's lack of restraint and forethought. He blindly rushes into a number of affairs and, had he but stopped to think for even a moment, he would easily have seen that the consequences of his actions could be disastrous. As Fielding phrases it, Tom's "animal spirits" are too high; they control and dominate his human rationality. Tom must find a way to reverse this balance, for that reversal, which occurs in the jail and is accompanied by sincere repentence for his past actions, is the key to his redemption. Further, the solution must occur within the framework of his society. As noted in the commentary on the Man of the Hill chapters, Fielding does not see isolation from humanity as a viable form of maintaining a virtuous existence. Virtue, as Fielding defines it, necessarily includes a continuous expression of the charity of love.

A further clue in this structure is that *sophia* is the Greek word for wisdom, and wisdom is the epitome of the rationality which Tom must develop. In this light, it becomes clear that Tom's story is also the story of man's quest for the redeeming knowledge which will re-establish his true relationship to his environment. Allworthy's final blessing on Tom is very much like an echo of the Creator's words, "Well done, thou good and faithful servant."

When Tom regains the proper balance between rationality and animal appetite, a similar restoration of order occurs in society. This concept of right order and right reason is thoroughly grounded in eighteenth-century thought and is directly related to the idea of the Chain of Being, according to which every one has his purpose and proper place in the natural world as ordained by God. One cannot help but notice that the end of the novel contains a picture of a perfected order. Although Tom may, in ethical terms, deserve his place as heir of Allworthy's estate, he is, legally and literally, Allworthy's nephew. Thus, there are no violations of the natural order even in this minor, legalistic point. After all, it could not be "paradise regained" if there were any violations, however minor; at the end of the novel, the threat of evil has been entirely removed. Tom, with his hard-won wisdom, resides in security in the natural, wholesome landscape of the country. The All-worthy-Western world, which so lately threatened to disrupt into chaos, is now carefully structured and a fit reflection of divine order. Regardless of Fielding's sarcasm and criticism, there can be no stronger indication of his complete faith in, and commitment to, man's rational powers.

NARRATIVE STYLE

After only two or three chapters of *Tom Jones,* the reader discovers that Fielding's style of narration varies tremendously with the subject at hand. One can, I think, make some worthwhile generalizations. First, *Tom Jones,* though actually intricately designed, gives the appearance of being randomly organized. The same is true of the style in which it is written; from the first chapter with its "menu metaphor," the style seems to be that of conversational ramble. Within these apparent ramblings, however, there is a delicate structure of irony on which the whole novel is precariously balanced. If the reader is lazy or inattentive to the subtleties of Fielding's style, the network collapses into a boring maze of incidents. *Tom Jones* demands the reader's full intellectual energies.

Fielding is a master stylist. He can range from the full, bawdy burlesque (as when Tom and Molly are in the thicket, or the scene with Squire Western's drunken rantings), to the simple, conversational style (which he uses in the introductions and a substantial portion of the narrative), to flights of ecstasy in the best heroic style (as in the introduction of Sophia or any of his various invocations to the muses). A brief example of these three basic styles will suffice to indicate the major tones of the novel.

Among other good uses for which I have thought proper to institute these several introductory chapters, I have considered them as a kind of mark or stamp, which may hereafter enable a very indifferent reader to distinguish what is true and genuine in this historic kind of writing, from what is false and counter-feit. Indeed, it seems likely that some such mark may shortly become necessary, since the favourable reception which two or three authors have lately procured for their works of this nature from the public, will probably serve as an encouragement to many others to undertake the like.

(Book IX, Chapter I)

It was now a pleasant evening in the latter end of June, when our hero was walking in a most delicious grove, where the gentle breezes fanning the leaves, together with the sweet trilling of a murmuring stream, and the melodious notes of nightingales, formed altogether the most enchanting harmony. In this scene, so sweetly accommodated to love, he meditated on his dear Sophia. . . . and his lively imagination painted the charming maid in various ravishing forms, his warm heart melted with tenderness . . . he started up, and beheld — not his Sophia . . . No; without a gown, in a shift that was somewhat of the coarsest, and none of the cleanest, bedewed likewise with some odoriferous effluvia, the produce of the day's labour, with a pitchfork in her hand, Molly Seagrim approached. . . . Here ensued a parley, which, as I do not think myself obliged to relate it, I shall omit it. It is sufficient that it lasted a full quarter of an hour at the conclusion of which they retired into the thickest part of the grove. . . . No sooner had our hero retired with his Dido, but . . . the parson and the young squire, who were taking a serious walk, arrived at the stile which leads into the grove, and the latter caught a view of the lovers just as they were sinking out of sight. . . . The way through which our hunters were to pass in pursuit of their game was so beset with briars, that it greatly obstructed their walk, and caused besides such a rustling that Jones had sufficient warning of their arrival . . . that he was (to use the language of sportsmen) found sitting. As in the season of *rutting* (an uncouth phrase, by which the vulgar denote that gentle dalliance, which in the well-wooded forest of Hampshire, passes between lovers of the ferine kind). . . . If, I say, while these sacred rites, which are common to *genus omne animantium,* are in agitation between the stag and his mistress, any hostile beasts should venture too near, on the first hint given by the frightened hind, fierce and tremendous rushes forth the stag to the entrance of the thicket; there stands he sentinel over his love, stamps the ground with his foot, and with his horns brandished aloft in the air, proudly provokes the apprehended foe to combat.

(Book V, Chapters X-XI)

The above passage is really so finely written that one cannot resist making a few comments upon it. First, one should go back and reread the two chapters in their entirety, for after so doing, what first appears to be sheer verbiage is in reality a device which Fielding uses to greatly retard the motion of the narrative so that the reader can relish with full enjoyment the image which the scene presents. Second, the passage is highlighted by another relatively frequent device which Fielding uses to add delight to his comic passages — the pun. When Tom and Molly go into the grove, Fielding states that "our hero advanced with his Dido." Now Dido is the name of a lovely, mythical Roman lady, the lover of Aeneas; but it is also very close in sound to the now archaic word "dildo," which refers to the male sexual organ and which was familiar enough to Fielding's contemporaries. Also, in the simile of the stag and doe, Fielding states that the stag, upon the intrusion of hostile parties, stands with "his horns brandished aloft." Horns are, of course, the primary symbol for the cuckolded husband or lover and, since Tom's companion on this occasion is Molly, the symbol is most apt. This is the kind of subtle detail so prevalent in Fielding's writing which makes his style so thoroughly delightful and which demands the reader's close attention. Let us now, however, move on to the third example of Fielding's style.

> The shadows began now to descend larger from the high mountains; the feathered creation had betaken themselves to their rest. Now the highest order of mortals were sitting down to their dinners, and the lowest order to their suppers. In a word, the clock struck five just as Mr. Jones took his leave of Gloucester; an hour at which (as it was now mid-winter) the dirty fingers of Night would have drawn her sable curtain over the universe had not the moon forbid her, who now, with a face as broad and as red as those of some jolly mortals, who, like her, turn night into day, began to rise from her bed, where she had slumbered away the day, in order to sit up all night. Jones had not travelled far before he paid his compliments to that beautiful planet, and, turning to his companion, asked him if he had ever beheld so delicious an evening? Partridge making no ready answer to his question, he proceeded to comment on the beauty of the moon, and repeated some passages from Milton, who hath certainly excelled all other poets in his description of the heavenly luminaries.
>
> (Book VIII, Chapter IX)

By far, the most outstanding aspect of Fielding's style is the recurrence of finely balanced passages of irony. These passages appear, generally speaking, in two different forms. One form is actually a juxtaposition of two passages in which a character first utters grand words about a noble philosophical idea, and then Fielding reveals the hypocrisy of the character by showing him acting in direct opposition to his so-called philosophy. He does this to Blifil throughout the novel; Blifil is by far the most thoroughly evil and hypocritical character. A variation upon this motif occurs when a character, again in stentorian tones, utterly condemns a particular vice and then immediately commits this vice. The Man of the Hill, for example, does this when he curses the world for its cruelty, and then refuses to help a person in distress. There are other variations on this reversal motif, but these examples serve to describe the broad outlines of the pattern.

The other kind of irony in *Tom Jones* is more difficult to describe. It occurs when the narrator is speaking directly to the reader and the irony and humor depend upon a certain progression which begins with seeming praise, or at least neutrality, but through the description of one element in a character, the whole passage becomes direct, unmitigated condemnation because it reveals the lack of a more essential element in that character. When Fielding is delving into the character of Mrs. Western, for example, he uses this technique.

> [Mrs. Western] was a lady of a different turn. She had lived about the court, and had seen the world. Hence, she had acquired all that knowledge the said world usually communicates; and was a perfect mistress of manners, customs, ceremonies, and fashions. Nor did her erudition stop here. She had considerably improved her mind by study; she had not only read all the modern plays, operas, oratorios, poems, and romances — in all which she was a critic; but had gone through Rapin's History of England, Eachard's Roman History, and many French *Memoires pour servir a l'Histoire:* to these she had added most of the political pamphlets and journals published within the last twenty years. . . . She was, moreover, excellently well skilled in the doctrine of Amour. . . . knowledge which she the more easily attained, as her pursuit of it was never diverted by any affairs of her own; for whether she had no inclinations, or they had never been solicited; which last is indeed very probable; . . . However, as she had considered the matter scientifically, she perfectly well knew, though she had never practised them, all the arts which fine ladies use when they desire to give encouragement, or to conceal liking, with all the long appendage of smiles, ogles, glances, etc., as they are at present practised in the beau-monde. To sum the whole, no species of disguise or affectation had escaped her notice; but as to the plain simple workings of honest nature, as she had never seen

any such, she could know but little of them.
(Book VI, Chapter II)

One should note the progression here. Fielding, by giving more and more evidence of the lady's store of knowledge, builds his praise to a climax. Then, with the concluding sentence, he destroys the framework upon which the praise is built by implying that this knowledge of disguise and affectation is totally useless because Mrs. Western has not "the plain simple workings of honest nature." The force of the criticism of Mrs. Western is particularly strong because "manners, customs, ceremonies, fashion" are juxtaposed with "plain simple honest nature"; deceit is plainly compared to sincerity. Further, as is quite often the case with Fielding, there is a double irony working here. Besides her concern with the intricacies of love, Mrs. Western is attempting to counsel both her brother and her niece on a subject of which she has had no experience, or at least no success, whatsoever.

Since *Tom Jones* is basically a novel of irony, the kind of writing described above accounts for a large portion of the work. Fielding's method of showing "the true ridiculous" is to compare it either implicitly or explicitly with the social and ethical norms which are almost universally espoused.

Another important stylistic element in *Tom Jones* is that Fielding constantly keeps the reader aware of the fact that he is reading a novel which is a work of art carefully constructed for certain ends. He does this through the guise of the objective narrator who discourses on the characters and directly addresses the reader. The introductory chapters are quite obvious examples of this; there, Fielding discusses the novel itself, as well as literary theories and critics, all of which directly concern the literary craftsmanship involved in *Tom Jones*. A second way in which Fielding draws attention to his artifice is through the chapter titles. One need only read through them to discover that they refer as much to the reader, author, and the mechanics of writing as they do to the plot: "Containing five pages of paper"; "A short hint of what we can do in the sublime"; "Being the shortest chapter in this Book"; "A battle sung by the Muse in the Homerican style"; "A short chapter containing a short dialogue"; and "Containing a portion of introductory writing."

Having made this observation, one must attempt to discover the reason for this practice. Obviously, it is in keeping with the tone of the novel, for in many of the chapter titles the author directs his wit at himself; the titles become quite funny because they are totally unexpected.

More important, the effect of this device is to posit another level of awareness. In most realistic novels, the reader is asked to engage in what Samuel Coleridge calls a "willing suspension of disbelief"; that is, the reader is asked to believe for the duration of the novel, that the experiences presented therein are as valid as any which have actually occurred. Fielding, however, does not set up this requirement; from the outset, he makes us aware of our role as reader and of himself as author. It is from this level of consciousness that we watch the history unfold. From such a point of view, one can concentrate on the moral framework and the subtle workings of both the plot and the style of the novel. In the eighteenth century, nearly all writers and critics believed that art should be both instructive and entertaining. Fielding accomplishes this task in a unique way; by emphasizing his art, as well as discussing ethics, Fielding forces his reader to use his rational, critical faculties instead of simply allowing himself to be caught up solely in the story.

One can fruitfully compare Fielding's techniques with those of the twentieth-century German playwright, Bertolt Brecht, who wrote what he called Epic Theater. One of Brecht's principal ideas was to employ alienation effects, which were supposed to keep the viewer aware that he was watching a play and to make him criticize the actor, the role, the action and the implied ethics so that after watching the play, the viewer would be motivated to act according to the ideals of social justice and human conduct inspired in him by his *own* objective, intellectual participation in the performance. Obviously, Fielding's techniques are neither as well articulated nor so conscientiously and strongly presented as Brecht's, but it is interesting to note that the roots of what is thought of as a revolutionary idea in theater in the early 1900s are present in Fielding's *Tom Jones,* written nearly two hundred years earlier. As Fielding himself stated in the dedicatory letter to Lyttleton, ". . . to recommend goodness and innocence hath been my sincere endeavour in this history . . . and to say the truth, it is likeliest to be attained in books of this kind; for an example is a kind of picture, in which virtue becomes, as it were, an object of sight, and strikes us with an idea of that loveliness, which Plato asserts there is in her naked charms." One further result of such a practice is that one is also guided into appreciating the art of the work for its own sake; one's attention is drawn to the form. Thus, he can observe the form as it is being fulfilled.

CHARACTERIZATION

One can safely state that in *Tom Jones* Fielding primarily uses two methods of characterization: action and authorial description. The two notable exceptions are the Man of the Hill and Mrs. Fitzpatrick, but even in these instances of narrated life histories, their stories are filled with choices and courses of action. In all cases, though, however much description we read, we always discover the true nature of a character through his deeds. Squire Allworthy, we are told, is the best of men; this is largely true, yet he does unjustly disinherit Tom and trust Thwackum, Square, and Blifil. Squire Western constantly professes his ardent love for Sophia, but he does mistreat her and demand that she marry the heir to the Allworthy estate, whoever it may be. One can go on in this vein for nearly every character in the novel. In the final analysis, one can once again detect Fielding's apprenticeship as a playwright because he depends very heavily on action to convey character.

Granting the importance of action, we have an apparent contradiction, because all of Fielding's characters are static. They do not grow and develop during the novel. With the possible exception of Tom, each character is the same person at the end of the novel that he was at the beginning. Throughout the novel, Fielding uses his own set of stock, humorous characters: the greedy landlord; the inept, pedantic tutor; the shrewish, domineering female; the cunning male suitor; and the silly, inconsequential nobleman. Since we see these same traits in numerous characters, the feeling of a static world is reinforced.

As far as the main characters are concerned, Fielding's key to characterization is that he emphasizes one particular trait in each one. Blifil is unscrupulous and greedy; Tom is lusty and rash; Squire Allworthy is just but gullible; Squire Western loves hunting and drinking; Mrs. Western is the self-styled expert on all subjects; Partridge is a bad Latin scholar, afraid of his own shadow; Sophia is innocent, honest, and sincere. One can go on and on, but the point is clear: Fielding has not attempted to draw fully rounded characters. Rather, he has infused a sense of the immediacy and vitality of life by a multiplicity of characters, nearly all of whom are representative of extremes so that the interactions between them are always pitched at an intense level. The rapidity with which the events flow, and with which characters move in and out of scenes, tends to distract our attention from the unifaceted nature of the characters. In effect, then, Fielding has substituted a multiplicity of characters for a character with a multiplicity of traits. Psychologically, this has its advantages; it allows the reader to see each trait in all of its glory or shame. It further serves to reinforce Fielding's point that one bad act or one bad trait does not make a villain; it simply makes a man human. And humanity, after all, is the subject of the novel, for the epigraph reads, *Mores hominum multorum vidit* ("he saw the manners of many men"). In presenting the manners which he has witnessed, Fielding burlesques the undesirable ones by making the characters caricatures.

FIELDING AND THE BEATLES

Despite the heading of this section, the following remarks do not represent a token gesture to the "now generation" in the form of a valiant attempt to make *Tom Jones* somehow relevant. Critics who make obvious and belabored attempts to prove how relevant a particular work of art is devalue both the work of art and the intelligence of their readers. A good work of art speaks powerfully of the human experience and is always relevant, provided that the reader allows himself to be receptive and permits his imagination to communicate with the imagination which produced the art. Rather, this section is included to indicate the universality of the ideas presented in *Tom Jones*. One of the most direct ways of illustrating this is by means of analogues, which are simply two or more similar stories that may or may not be directly related to each other.

In their 1967 album, "Magical Mystery Tour," the Beatles produced a rather fascinating analogue to the Man of the Hill section of *Tom Jones*. Their song "The Fool on the Hill" presents a character in a situation directly analogous to the Man of Mazard Hill; even the titles are similar. To refresh the reader's memory, "The Fool on the Hill" describes a misanthropic recluse who is disliked by the world because he sees the absurdity of their doomed society. The Fool is, of course, the archetypal sage, "the man with a foolish grin," who looks condescendingly down upon the greatly inferior mass of common, unenlightened humanity.

The similarities to the Man of the Hill are too great to miss. Both the Beatles' and Fielding's characters are physically and mentally isolated from the rest of society. They live alone on a hill, above the world, indicating a superior position. They both seem to have greater wisdom and understanding than the rest of the world. The Man of the Hill devotes his time to meditating on the ancient philosophers and criticizing the attitudes and actions of humanity; he proclaims the desperate straits of a cruel, unjust, thoughtless and selfish mass of animals. The Fool on the Hill also sees a gloomy world caught in its own trap; he "sees the sun going down and . . . the world spinning round." The image of the setting sun is, of course, an image of despair, for it signals the end of light, traditionally associated with knowledge, hope, and security, and the beginning of the fears, uncertainty, and darkness of night. The image of the spinning world is indicative of unending cycles dulling the senses and eroding the mind. Both characters, because of the position they have taken, inspire fear and dislike in others. The Man of the Hill's neighbors think he is mad and perhaps a demon and refuse to associate with him. The same is true of the Beatles' Fool: "Nobody wants to know him, they can see that he's just a fool . . . they don't like him." The reason behind this antipathy is that both characters stand for a way of life totally alien to the societal norm and, as such, they stand for a change in the basic societal structure. The Man of the Hill would have human nature changed to rid itself of its egocentricity. Though we know much less about the Fool on the Hill's ideology, we do know he would have drastic changes: "and nobody seems to like him, they can tell what he wants to do." In other words, from their way of life, the men are "talking perfectly loud" to any who will listen. But although they may ask many questions, the rest of the people do not wish to hear the answer they already know too well. For both "fools," this makes no difference; each is content to remain with his "head in a cloud," grinning his foolish but superior grin.

There are, however, two major differences between the two characters. The first concerns the kind of knowledge that the characters have. The Man of the Hill has gained his knowledge of human behavior through his own experience, however limited, and has gained what wisdom he thinks he has through studying the ancient sages. The Fool on the Hill has knowledge of quite a different kind, as is readily evident when "The Fool on the Hill" is placed in its proper context in the album. The "mystery tour" of the album's title and the first song is a tour through the mind under the influence of drugs. The first words of the album are, "Roll up, roll up for the Mystery Tour," which can quite easily be interpreted as an invitation to "roll up a joint." The third band on the record, "Blue Jay Way," is even more obvious. The music, with its background of sustained, rather atonal glissando effects, is evocative of the magic of a hallucinogenic drug experience. The song opens with a reference to a fog in which "my friends have lost their way." But this is obviously neither ordinary fog nor ordinary geographical disorientation, for the singers state, "We'll be over soon, they said. Now they've lost *themselves* instead." The remainder of the song is but a request to the singers' friends to "don't be long for I may be asleep." Similar to this fog and sleep imagery, the Fool on the Hill is "well on the way, head in a cloud."

The kind of isolation maintained by the Fool results in a polarized, we-they world. Those who share the Fool's wisdom experience a strong sense of mystical unity. The first line of the album's final song, "I am the Walrus," clearly states this: "I am he as you are he as you are me and we are together." But opposed to this "we" are the outsiders: "they," the participants in what used to be called "the rat race." The refrain of "Blue Jay Way" actually prepares the listener for this polarization, because the singer's repeated admonition to his friends to hurry, to "don't be long," quickly begins to sound like "don't belong." "They" are further represented by the mother in "Your Mother Should Know," who "was born a long, long time ago" and who obviously does belong. The compatriots of The Fool on the Hill maintain their isolation, their purity of experience by continual change so that the rest of the uninitiated world does not intrude by simply imitating the superficial aspects of their experience. Thus, the limits of extremity are extended as "they" catch on: "I am the eggman, they are the eggmen—I am the Walrus." In essence, then, the Fool on the Hill is the silent spokesman for a clique of truthseekers who have found an answer. With Fielding's Man of the Hill, the same kind of polarization has occurred, but his rejection is much more complete; he has no circle of other hermits and he extends no invitations. He has rejected not just society's ideology but mankind itself. The world of the Man of the Hill is totally narcissistic; he experiences union only with nature and himself. The Man of the Hill is essentially anti-human while the Fool on the Hill seems to represent a movement toward human unity through the experience of drugs which somehow bring on instant apocalypse and the establishment of an ideal world.

The second major difference between these two hill-dwellers is that of their author's attitude toward them. As was discussed at length in the commentary on Book VIII, Fielding obviously strongly disapproves of both the isolation and the attitude of the Man of the Hill. The Beatles, however, show no such disapproval; in fact, the remainder of the songs on the album reinforce the necessity for rejecting societal norms which dictate that "man, you been a naughty boy; you let your face grow long." The fragility of such a society is reflected in the image, "sitting on a cornflake," which is indeed a precarious position. Also, "The Fool on the Hill" ends with an affirmation of the Fool's position and the validity of his vision: "He knows that *they*'re the fools."

The significance of these differences is that they are indicative of more profound differences in both the cultural values and individual world views of the authors. Drug experimentation simply was not prevalent in eighteenth-century England. More important, Fielding's rejection of the misanthropic hermit reflects his broad faith in both the individual man and in the ability of societal institutions to serve the individual's needs equitably while maintaining the order of reason. In other words, Fielding is establishment-oriented; Allworthy, though he has his faults, is the good, just man who works within the framework of society and accomplishes much that is beneficial. At the end of the novel, Tom Jones is also an establishment man with estate, family, and social position. He is becoming another Allworthy. Fielding's own life is consistent with this view, for he attempted to correct, not to by-pass or destroy, social institutions. The Beatles' acceptance of the Fool on the Hill and their portrait of polarization indicate a rejection of the establishment in favor of individual liberty. One hardly need comment on their expression of their own individuality. Their faith is in the individual man, not in mankind.

The image of the self-exiled wise man is actually quite common in English literature. The closest parallel to Fielding's Man of the Hill is Lemuel Gulliver. Near the close of *Gulliver's Travels,* he, like the Man of the Hill, has become totally embittered toward man and can see no worth in him. He rejects all social intercourse and speaks only to his horses; in other words, he has become a fool. Swift illustrates Gulliver's foolishness in the same way that Fielding illustrates that of the Man of the Hill: by presenting good, honest, and generous men *within* the society. Their message of hope is based on a faith in man's ability to rectify his errors and to improve, if not perfect, his society. The Beatles, looking at a far more complex and potentially far more evil society, place their faith in man's ability to fulfill himself; they ignore the impersonal and repressive institutions of a society which has lost all guiding faith and retains only the empty shell of frantic activity.

REVIEW QUESTIONS

1. After examining several appropriately different passages in *Tom Jones,* discuss the ways in which Fielding's style changes with the subject matter. What effects do such changes in style achieve?

2. Discuss Fielding's *methods* of characterization in *Tom Jones.* Are all the major characters equally "life-like"? What reasons can you suggest for this inequality?

3. It is obvious that Fielding is satirizing certain flaws in human nature, namely pretension to wisdom and virtue. This trait appears in

a number of characters. After analyzing several such characters, suggest some reasons why an author would engage in this kind of redundancy.

4. Fielding uses yet another kind of redundancy. As soon as Tom has left Somersetshire, he meets a Quaker who tells the story of his daughter, a tale that is very much like the story of Sophia Western. Does this kind of repetition serve any useful purpose? If so, what?

5. One characteristic of *Tom Jones* is its topicality; that is, Fielding refers, sometimes at length, to issues which though controversial enough in 1749, have lost much of their interest. Is this necessary in a work of art? Why or why not? What are the disadvantages and advantages of employing this technique?

6. There are numerous occasions when Fielding describes the setting of the action quite thoroughly. Discuss the possible purposes of such lengthy description. How does the setting in *Tom Jones* contribute to thematic development?

7. Fielding frequently informs us of what the surrounding neighborhood thinks of particular events or actions. What part, if any, does this chorus of opinion play in the novel?

8. The nature of irony is that one says exactly the opposite of what he means; thus, in using it, an author runs the risk of being misunderstood. Yet Fielding employs it frequently throughout *Tom Jones*. Why would an artist, sincerely attempting to make moral statements, run this risk? What is to be gained through effectively used irony? Is Fielding's irony effective? Why or why not?

9. Define the word "digression" and discuss its relevance to the introductory chapters and, particularly, Book VIII of *Tom Jones*.

10. Discuss the importance of such a highly involved and complicated plot as that of *Tom Jones*. How are plot and setting related to the moral structure of the novel? In answering this question, one would do well to consider Fielding's remarks at the beginning of Book IX, Chapter 1.

11. Discuss Fielding's attitude toward the Aristotelian concept of imitating nature. Is this related to his insistence on an artist's or critic's need for experience? Is Fielding's work a picture of "reality"? Does

the conclusion of the novel mar Fielding's achievement along these lines? If so, what justification can you advance for Fielding's using this kind of conclusion?

12. If *Tom Jones* is realistic, how then can it also be allegorical or, at least, contain representative characters?

13. In *Tom Jones*, Fielding quotes copiously from various authors. What is his purpose in doing so?

14. Considering several contemporary novels which you have read, construct a definition of the novel. Now compare your definition with *Tom Jones*, pointing out similarities and differences. From this basis, make several observations about the development of the novel, remembering that Fielding's efforts helped to establish the genre.

15. From other novels, drama or poetry that you have read, can you see any analogues to *Tom Jones?* What similarities indicate that the analogue may have been inspired by a section of *Tom Jones?* What are the major differences between the analogue and *Tom Jones?* What is the significance of these differences?

BIBLIOGRAPHY

ALTER, ROBERT. *Fielding and the Nature of the Novel.* Cambridge: Harvard University Press, 1968. A very thorough and helpful discussion of the function of style, character, and architectonics in Fielding's novels, with particular emphasis on *Tom Jones* and *Joseph Andrews.* The first chapter is a refutation of critics, from Samuel Johnson to F. R. Leavis, who have dismissed Fielding's work as unimportant.

BATTESTIN, MARTIN, ed. *Twentieth Century Interpretations of "Tom Jones."* Englewood Cliffs, New Jersey: Prentice-Hall, Inc., 1968. A very useful collection of critical essays with a good cross section of viewpoints from prominent critics in the field.

BLANCHARD, FREDERIC T. *Fielding the Novelist: A Study in Historical Criticism.* New Haven: Yale University Press, 1926. A tiring but informative and well-documented study of Fielding's reputation.

DUDDEN, HOMES. *Henry Fielding: His Life, Work, and Times.* 2 vols. London: Oxford University Press, 1952. A study of Fielding's works in relation to the author and his social milieu.

EHRENPREIS, IRVING. *Fielding: "Tom Jones."* London: Edward Arnold, Ltd., 1964. A good, brief study, with some excellent comments on the author's presence and tone of voice in the novel.

GOLDEN, MORRIS. *Fielding's Moral Psychology.* Amherst, Mass.: University of Massachusetts Press, 1966. A study of the ethical system in Fielding's novels, centering on the tension between the self and society. Morris relates this tension to the same tension between the philosophies of Locke and Shaftesbury.

HATFIELD, GLENN W. *Henry Fielding and the Language of Irony.* Chicago: University of Chicago Press, 1968. A stimulating book on irony. The two final chapters are on *Tom Jones* and concern Fielding's concept of "prudence" and the effect of "dramatized authorship."

HUTCHENS, ELEANOR N. *Irony in "Tom Jones."* University, Alabama: University of Alabama Press, 1964. This makes an interesting contrast with Hatfield's book, for it too concerns the uses of irony and the theme of "prudence" in *Tom Jones.*

JOHNSON, MAURICE. *Fielding's Art of Fiction.* Philadelphia: University of Pennsylvania Press, 1961. A general survey of Fielding's accomplishments in fiction. It examines in some detail all of his prose works.

PAULSON, RONALD, ed. *Fielding: A Collection of Critical Essays.* Twentieth Century Views Series. Englewood Cliffs, New Jersey: Prentice-Hall, 1962. This volume contains essays on individual novels (five on *Tom Jones*), as well as two more general essays, one on Fielding's irony and one on his artistic techniques.

SACKS, SHELDON. *Fiction and the Shape of Belief: A Study of Fielding, with Glances at Swift, Johnson, and Richardson.* Berkeley: University of California Press, 1964. Beginning with a formal analysis of the types of fiction, Sacks discusses Fielding's structures and the way in which the beliefs of an author inevitably become part of his artistic creations.

RAWSON, C. J. *Henry Fielding*. London: Routledge & Kegan Paul, Ltd., 1968. This is a series of extracts from various of Fielding's prose works, including the preface to *Joseph Andrews*. It contains rather helpful and illuminating short commentaries and footnotes.

WATT, IAN. *The Rise of the Novel: Studies in Defoe, Richardson, and Fielding*. Berkeley: University of California Press, 1957. An important book on the development of the novel, with lucid and sometimes controversial views of each of these early practitioners. For an interesting contrast, one should consult a book which is similar in scope and published about the same time: ALAN D. MCKILLOP. *The Early Masters of English Fiction*. Lawrence, Kansas: University of Kansas, 1956.

WRIGHT, ANDREW. *Henry Fielding: Mask and Feast*. Berkeley: University of California Press, 1965. A study of the structural coherence of Fielding's works, with useful comments concerning influences on Fielding and comparisons of Fielding's achievements with his predecessors.